GUIDE TO
GREEN
BUILDING
RATING
SYSTEMS

GUIDE TO
GREEN
BUILDING
RATING
SYSTEMS

Understanding LEED,
Green Globes, ENERGY STAR,
the National Green Building
Standard, and More

LINDA REEDER

WILEY

John Wiley & Sons, Inc.

Published by John Wiley & Sons, Inc., Hoboken, New Jersey

Published simultaneously in Canada.

For general information about our other products and services, please contact our Customer Care Department within the United States at (800) 762-2974, outside the United States at (317) 572-3993, or fax (317) 572-4002.

Wiley also publishes its books in a variety of electronic formats. Some content that appears in print may not be available in electronic books. For more information about Wiley products, visit our web site at www.wiley.com.

Library of Congress Cataloging-in-Publication Data:

Reeder, Linda.
   Guide to rating green buildings / Linda Reeder.
       p. cm.
   Includes bibliographical references and index.
   ISBN 978-0-470-40194-1 (pbk.)
   1. Sustainable buildings—Evaluation. 2. Sustainable construction—Standards.   I. Title.
   TH880.R43 2010
       720'.47—dc22   2009036485

Printed in the United States of America

10 9 8 7 6 5 4 3 2 1

CONTENTS

ACKNOWLEDGMENTS

I AM VERY GRATEFUL to all the architects, builders, construction managers, designers, developers, engineers, owners, representatives of rating systems, and the marketing professionals who support them, all of whom gave generously of their time and expertise to make this book possible. Their commitment to creating a sustainable built environment has been inspiring to me. I am also indebted to the talented photographers and kind copyright holders who allowed their images to be included in the pages that follow.

Special thanks are owed to Barbara Nadel, FAIA, my former editor-in-chief at AIA Soloso, who encouraged me to undertake this project; Richard Hayes, AIA, the Managing Director of AIA Knowledge Resources, who initially suggested that I investigate different green building rating systems; and my editor John Czarnecki at John Wiley & Sons, Inc. for giving me the opportunity and helping me focus this project and keep it on track.

Finally, I would like to thank Christopher Anderson for everything.

LINDA REEDER
New Haven, Connecticut

INTRODUCTION

Concerns about climate change and interest in sustainable design affect all segments of the building industry. Owners—including homeowners, developers, corporations, and local government entities—often want an environmentally friendly building but do not fully understand what this entails. Building professionals who are asked to design and build sustainable buildings may first need to help their clients define their goals for sustainability before moving forward with projects. Meeting the requirements of a rating system provides owners with a metric for evaluating their investment while helping design teams and constructors set priorities.

The number of rating systems has increased as the market for green buildings has grown. Rating systems that verify and quantify sustainable design and construction were once seen by owners as an unrecoverable and unnecessary cost; now they are viewed as guidelines, marketing tools, and a way to lower operating costs. This book, *Guide to Green Building Rating Systems,* is intended to help owners, constructors, and design teams select the appropriate national rating system for their projects. It describes rating systems for both residential and commercial new construction, including LEED®, Green Globes™, ENERGY STAR®, and the National Green Building Standard™.

The book begins with an overview of the most widely used rating systems and compares key features such as cost, ease of use, and building performance. The remainder of the guide is divided into two sections, one on single- and multifamily residential construction (Chapters 3–7) and one on nonresidential construction (Chapters 8–12). Each rating system is examined in detail, including its evolution, objectives, criteria, levels of certification, benefits, and shortcomings. For each rating system, a series of case studies representing diverse project types, sizes, certification levels, and climate regions illustrates the application of the rating system under discussion. Case studies include "lessons learned" from designers, builders, and owners. Less well-known national, local, regional, and international rating systems are also addressed.

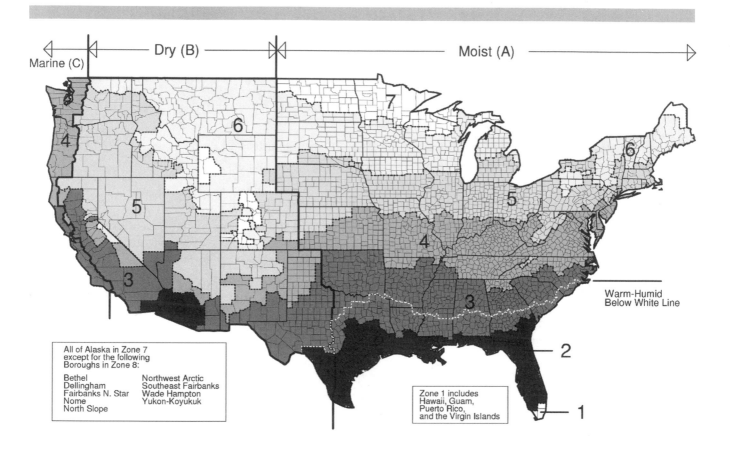

Figure 0-1 The climate zones shown here are referenced in building case studies throughout this book. *Image courtesy of 2006 International Energy Conservation Code, Copyright 2006. Washington, DC: International Code Council. Reproduced with permission. All rights reserved. www.iccsafe.org.*

CLIMATE ZONES

The local climate plays an important role in determining which optional elements of a national rating system are most pertinent to a particular project. In the case studies in this book, the climate zone listed is as presented on the 2006 International Energy Conservation Code map of climate regions (shown here) and the corresponding list of climate zones, by county. The U.S. Department of Energy (DOE)'s definitions of climate regions are based on heating degree-days, average temperatures, and precipitation, and are described here.

Hot-Humid

A hot-humid climate is generally defined as a region that receives more than 20 inches (50 cm) of annual precipitation and where one or both of the following occur:

- A 67°F (19.5°C) or higher wet bulb temperature for 3,000 or more hours during the warmest six consecutive months of the year; or

- A 73°F (23°C) or higher wet bulb temperature for 1,500 or more hours during the warmest six consecutive months of the year.

Mixed-Humid

A mixed-humid climate is generally defined as a region that receives more than 20 inches (50 cm) of annual precipitation, has approximately 5,400 heating degree-days (65°F basis) or fewer, and where the average monthly outdoor temperature drops below 45°F (7°C) during the winter months.

Hot-Dry

A hot-dry climate is generally defined as a region that receives less than 20 inches (50 cm) of annual precipitation and where the monthly average outdoor temperature remains above 45°F (7°C) throughout the year.

Mixed-Dry

A mixed-dry climate is generally defined as a region that receives less than 20 inches (50 cm) of annual precipitation, has approximately 5,400 heating degree-days (50°F basis) or fewer, and where the average monthly outdoor temperature drops below 45°F (7°C) during the winter months.

Cold

A cold climate is generally defined as a region with approximately 5,400 heating degree-days (65°F basis) or more, and fewer than approximately 9,000 heating degree-days (65°F basis).

Very Cold

A very cold climate is generally defined as a region with approximately 9,000 heating degree-days (65°F basis) or more, and fewer than approximately 12,600 heating degree-days (65°F basis).

Subarctic

A subarctic climate is generally defined as a region with approximately 12,600 heating degree-days (65°F basis) or more.

Marine

A marine climate is generally defined as a region that meets all of the following criteria:

- A mean temperature of coldest month between 27°F (−3°C) and 65°F (18°C).
- A warmest month mean of less than 72°F (22°C).
- At least four months with mean temperatures higher than 50°F (10°C).
- A dry season in summer. The month with the heaviest precipitation in the cold season has at least three times as much precipitation as the month with the least precipitation in the rest of the year. The cold season is October through March in the northern hemisphere and April through September in the southern hemisphere.

This book does not describe strategies for achieving sustainable design and construction, as many other publications do so well; nor does it make a case for the importance of green building. It focuses instead on national rating systems that provide the metrics to evaluate sustainable design and construction. Each system is described clearly and thoroughly, to be readily understandable to someone with no experience with the system. At the same time, chapters are organized so that readers with some familiarity with the rating system can easily identify and locate information that is new to them.

A NOTE ON "GREEN" TERMINOLOGY

The terms "green," "sustainable," and "high performance," when used to describe buildings, have different shades of meaning to some. For the purposes of this book, however, they are used interchangeably. This use is consistent with the U.S. Environmental Protection Agency's definition of green building as "the practice of creating structures and using processes that are environmentally responsible and resource-efficient throughout a building's life-cycle, from siting to design, construction, operation, maintenance, renovation, and deconstruction. This practice expands and complements the classical building design concerns of economy, utility, durability, and comfort. A green building is also known as a sustainable or high-performance building."[1]

NOTE

1. www.epa.gov/greenbuilding/pubs/about.htm; accessed February 24, 2009.

1

RESIDENTIAL RATING SYSTEMS: A COMPARISON

The four residential rating systems described in detail in this book were selected because of their national scope, acceptance in the construction industry, and not-for-profit origins. The rating systems provide the option for builders, owners, and designers to establish a metric verifying the relative greenness of their homes. This chapter gives a brief overview of ENERGY STAR® for Homes, LEED® for Homes, the NAHB Model Green Home Building Guidelines, and the National Green Building Standard™, as well as a comparison of key features. Later chapters offer a more in-depth look, along with illustrative case studies for each rating system. Information on Green Globes®, a commercial rating system that may be used for multifamily residential projects of more than three stories, can be found in Chapters 2 and 9.

BRIEF OVERVIEW OF RESIDENTIAL RATING SYSTEMS

ENERGY STAR for Homes

ENERGY STAR for Homes is a voluntary program of the U.S. Environmental Protection Agency (EPA) with the goal of market transformation. Cost-effectiveness is a core principle, and the EPA developed the program with the intent that any additional costs incurred by meeting the ENERGY STAR for Homes requirements be offset by the resulting savings in reduced energy costs.

The emphasis of ENERGY STAR for Homes is energy efficiency. Homes are rated on a 100-point index of energy performance. Beginning in 2011, indoor air quality measures are also required. LEED for Homes and the National Green Building Standard both reference ENERGY STAR for Homes in their rating systems.

LEED for Homes

LEED (Leadership in Energy in Environmental Design) for Homes is a program of the U.S. Green Building Council (USGBC), a nonprofit organization that launched its first green building rating system, a pilot program for commercial buildings, in 1998. LEED for Homes, officially launched in 2008, is a voluntary system that promotes the design and construction of green homes.[1] Sustainable criteria include site selection and development, water efficiency, and materials, as well as energy efficiency and indoor environmental quality. There are 136 points available in addition to mandatory prerequisites.

NAHB Model Green Home Building Guidelines

The National Association of Home Builders (NAHB), a trade association with the mission of enhancing the climate for housing and the building industry, developed the voluntary NAHB Model Green Home Building Guidelines for the mainstream home builder in 2005. The guidelines' sustainable criteria include lot design and development, resource efficiency, energy efficiency, water efficiency, indoor environmental quality, operation and homeowner education, and global impact. A range of points are available, depending on project specifics, up to about 867.

National Green Building Standard

The National Green Building Standard (ICC 700-2008) was developed by the NAHB Research Center in partnership with the International Code Council (ICC), which used the NAHB Green Home Building Guidelines as a starting point. It was approved by the American National Standards Institute (ANSI) in 2009. There are more than 1,000 points available in addition to some mandatory items.

ELIGIBILITY

While all four rating systems may be applied to new single-family homes, not all encompass multifamily and renovation projects (see Table 1-1).

TABLE 1-1 PROJECT TYPES ELIGIBLE FOR CERTIFICATION

	ENERGY STAR for Homes	LEED for Homes	NAHB Model Green Home Building Guidelines	National Green Building Standard
Single-Family New Construction	✓	✓	✓	✓
Single-Family Major Renovation	✓(1)	✓(1)		✓
Multifamily New Construction	✓(2)	✓(3)		✓
Multifamily Major Renovation	✓(1)(2)	✓(1)(2)	.	✓

(1) Exterior framing must be exposed to meet verification requirements for insulation and air sealing.
(2) Up to three stories. In 2009, ENERGY STAR had a pilot program underway for multifamily projects more than three stories high.
(3) Up to six stories high.

MARKET PENETRATION AND BRAND RECOGNITION

One reason builders and developers elect to build green homes is to gain a market advantage. Certification with a third-party rating system can demonstrate to potential buyers that a level of sustainability has been achieved. Buyer awareness of a specific rating system also may be seen as advantageous by owners, designers, or builders.

In the new homes sector in 2008, ENERGY STAR for Homes achieved an average national market presence of nearly 17 percent, up from 12 percent in 2007.[2] Since the ENERGY STAR rating can be earned by products like appliances and televisions as well as homes, many people are familiar with it: 76 percent of households recognized the ENERGY STAR label when shown it.[3] The oldest home rating system, more homes by far have received the ENERGY STAR label than the other systems discussed here, as shown in Table 1-2.

Although LEED for Homes was officially launched in 2008, the LEED brand dates back a decade earlier. LEED for New Construction is arguably the dominant commercial building rating system in the United States. As a brand name, LEED is well-known to many architects and other commercial building professionals, including institutional owners.

The NAHB Model Green Home Building Guidelines was developed for homebuilders and the National Green Building Standard (NGBS) adapted from these guidelines. Prepared for and marketed to homebuilders, it seems fair to assume that these rating systems appeal to homebuilders. As an organization, the NAHB is active in lobbying and other public activities, and so might have name recognition among some homebuyers.

TABLE 1-2 MARKET PENETRATION

	ENERGY STAR for Homes	LEED for Homes	NAHB Model Green Home Building Guidelines	National Green Building Standard
Year Launched	1995	2006[4]	2008[5]	2009
Number of Homes Certified	940,000 single-family homes(1)	2,566(2)	321(3)	19(3)

(1) As of July 2, 2009.[6]
(2) As of July 6, 2009.[7]
(3) As July 31, 2009.[8]

Figure 1-1 Awnings like these on Frank Lloyd Wright's Westcott House in Springfield, Ohio, have been reducing solar gain since well before "green" was a type of building. *Photo © 2007, Joseph M. Knapp.*

RATING BUILDING PERFORMANCE

With the exception of ENERGY STAR for Homes, the rating systems discussed here cover similar sustainable categories, as shown in Table 1-3. Whereas ENERGY STAR for Homes, LEED for Homes, and the National Green Building Standard are periodically reviewed and updated, the NAHB Model Green Home Building Guidelines will not be updated.[9] As a result, as green building practices advance, certification under the guidelines may become a less meaningful measure of home performance.

Climate affects priorities for building performance. ENERGY STAR for Homes has different prescriptive requirements for different climate regions. LEED for Homes offers up to four bonus points to increase the weight of regionally important credits. Although the NAHB Model Green Home Building Guidelines does not offer any incentives for regionally appropriate technologies, it has been adapted by some state homebuilders associations to their local climates. The National Green Building Standard addresses local climatic conditions in its Energy Efficiency category.

Building performance can be improved by looking at a house as a whole system rather than as individual components. For example, the home's orientation and building envelope will have an impact on the demands on an HVAC system. ENERGY STAR for Homes requires a plan review prior to construction, and LEED for Homes requires integrated project planning.

TABLE 1-3 CATEGORY TYPES CONSIDERED IN RATING BUILDING PERFORMANCE

	ENERGY STAR for Homes	LEED for Homes	NAHB Model Green Home Building Guidelines	National Green Building Standard
Site Selection		✓	✓	✓
Site Development		✓	✓	✓
Energy Efficiency	✓	✓	✓	✓
Water Conservation		✓	✓	✓
Material and Resource Efficiency		✓	✓	✓
Indoor Environmental Quality	✓(1)	✓	✓	✓
Owner/Tenant Education		✓	✓	✓
Other		Innovation and Design	Global Impact	

(1) Optional for homes permitted before January 1, 2011.

There is no requirement in the NAHB Model Green Home Building Guidelines or the National Green Building Standard to have a whole-home systems review prior to construction, although builders may choose to do so.

To qualify for certification, third-party verification is required for each system. Independent verifiers who have no financial stake in the project review documents and inspect construction to ensure measures have been implemented. Verification is as follows:

- *ENERGY STAR for Homes:* Plan review, construction inspections, and performance testing by a certified home energy rater or Building Option Package inspector is required to earn the ENERGY STAR label. When needed, energy modeling services are also provided by raters.

- *LEED for Homes:* Verification of certain mandatory items and other points by an approved third-party is required for LEED for Homes certification. This includes review of documentation, two on-site inspections, and performance testing.

- *NAHB Model Green Home Building Guidelines:* Verification of certain items by an approved third party is a requirement of certification. This includes two on-site inspections, as well as reviews of documentation.

- *National Green Building Standard:* The entity that adopts the standard determines how compliance is verified. Where the NGBS is not adopted but is used as a rating system, the NAHB Research Center's approved verifiers can provide verification services, which include two on-site inspections, as well as reviews of documentation.

EASE OF USE

A potential barrier to designers, builders, and developers using a rating system is the amount of time and effort required to learn about and implement it. While many may recognize the importance of having a metric to determine relative building performance and a certificate or label to confirm green building achievements, resources are often limited. Becoming familiar with any new rating system takes time, and it may take more time for some systems than others. The following list describes the relative ease of use of each system.

- *ENERGY STAR for Homes:* This rating system is a good one to start with, for several reasons:
  - It has a narrow focus, concentrating on energy efficiency. This focus will allow a user new to green building to learn the most important aspect of green building well. Energy efficiency has a great impact on the environment and also lowers operating costs.

- ENERGY STAR specifications are available for different climates, to help ensure energy efficiency requirements are met.

- For a home to qualify for the ENERGY STAR, a third-party inspector or rater must review the drawings for compliance. After the review, this rater can recommend improvements and construction practices to help ensure the home reaches the ENERGY STAR level. Designers or builders can rely on the expertise of the mandatory rater as they become familiar with the requirements.

- Cost-effectiveness is built into the system.

- ENERGY STAR is a component of and complements other residential rating systems, making it a gateway to rating systems that address a broader range of sustainability issues.

- *NAHB Model Green Home Building Guidelines:* The next step in the progression is the guidelines, for the following reasons:

  - With more than 800 points available, there are many options to choose from and very few mandatory items.

  - Since the guidelines were designed to be used by mainstream homebuilders,[10] they should be accessible to that audience.

  - In some cases, the guidelines describe a specific action needed to earn a credit, making their implementation easy for a novice to understand.

  - The NAHB Green Scoring Tool, available for free use at www.nahbgreen.org, offers links to resources relevant to implementing the credit. Note, however, that it can be time-consuming to score a home with the tool.

- *LEED for Homes and the National Green Building Standard:* These two systems are roughly comparable in terms of requirements and ease of use, and are more rigorous in terms of building performance than the previous two systems. Both have mandatory requirements and both require performance testing and have point thresholds in several categories. They have similar sustainable performance targets and offer parallel levels of certification. Of course, there are some differences, including:

  - More total points are available in NGBS than in LEED for Homes (as shown in Table 1-4), with points per credit typically having a greater value. The relative weight of categories is different, too.

  - As a proportion of total points available, LEED for Homes has more mandatory measures.

  - LEED for Homes requires the involvement of the Green Rater (verifier) during the project planning process, with the intent to "maximize opportunities for integrated, cost-effective adoption of green design

TABLE 1-4 POINT SYSTEMS

	ENERGY STAR for Homes	LEED for Homes	NAHB Model Green Home Building Guidelines	National Green Building Standard
Levels of Certification	1	4	3	4
Total Points Available	100-point index	136	Varies, from about 582 to 867	Varies, up to more than 1,000
Minimum Points Required for Certification	85 percent	45	237	222
Point Minimums per Category?	N/A	Yes(1)	Yes	Yes

(1) In select categories.

and construction strategies."[11] This early collaboration is not required by the NGBS, which could result in lower verification fees for a team experienced in green design and construction.

■ The NAHB Green Scoring Tool, available for free use at www.nahbgreen.org, generates a score sheet that can be converted to an Excel file and sent to the verifier—although, as noted previously, it can be time-consuming to score a home with the tool. As of 2009, LEED for Homes did not have an online tool for scoring and documentation, although a checklist may be downloaded.

Figure 1-2 Solar panels on this California home will contribute to a savings of 60 percent on utility bills for this net-zero energy home. *Photo courtesy of DOE/NREL.*

Figure 1-3 Drilling boreholes for a ground source heat pump system, also known as a geothermal heat pump system. This is a highly efficient renewable energy system for space heating and cooling and for water heating. *Photo courtesy of Ideal Homes, www.Ideal-Homes.com.*

COSTS OF COMPLIANCE

Many of the additional costs of building in compliance with a rating system are difficult to compare, for several reasons. These include the different credits that may be selected within each rating system and the variety of homes—in terms of climate, market, size, design complexity, and other variables—which make a straightforward cost comparison problematic. The fixed costs for each rating system are listed in Table 1-5.

Fees for the third-party verifier or rater vary as well, depending on factors such as project size, location, and certification level sought. Verifiers for all systems are independent contractors that set their own fees based on these variables. In 2008, the NAHB Research Center estimated plan review and verification costs for the NAHB Model Green Home Building Guidelines and the draft version of the National Green Building Standard at $750 per home for up to 10 homes.[12] Verification for ENERGY STAR homes typically will be less, since only energy efficiency is evaluated. For LEED for Homes, verification typically will be higher, because the green rater is included during the design process.

TABLE 1-5 REGISTRATION AND CERTIFICATION FEES(1) FOR A SINGLE-FAMILY HOME

	ENERGY STAR for Homes	LEED for Homes	NAHB Model Green Home Building Guidelines	National Green Building Standard
Registration (Members)	$0	$150	N/A	N/A
Registration (Nonmembers)	$0	$225	N/A	N/A
Certification (Members)	$0	$225	$200	$200
Certification (Nonmembers)	$0	$300	$500	$500

(1) Fees current as of July 2009.

Depending on options pursued, an energy model, which is a computer simulation of anticipated energy use based on the home design, might be required. The cost for this service varies depending on home size and other factors.

Finally, there may be extra construction costs for implementing the measures needed to obtain certification, depending on credits pursued and the standard features and quality of a builder's baseline nonrated home. Additional staff and subcontractor time may be necessary to learn about the rating system and how to meet requirements for certification.

PROFESSIONAL DESIGNATION

There are professional designations available that indicate either a level of expertise in green building, in a rating system, or both. ENERGY STAR has ENERGY STAR Partners, companies that participate in ENERGY STAR by building or designing ENERGY STAR qualified homes.

For LEED, a LEED AP (Accredited Professional) Homes designation is awarded to individuals who pass the LEED AP Homes exam. Exam candidates must have experience on a LEED project within the previous three years. The accrediting organization describes a LEED AP as someone who "possesses the knowledge and skills necessary to participate in the design process, to support and encourage integrated design, and to streamline the [LEED] application and certification process."[13]

The NAHB offers individuals a Certified Green Professional™ designation, which requires NAHB-approved training, including the two-day course, "Green Building for Building Professionals." The course discusses strategies for integrating green home building strategies without driving up construction costs and describes the benefits of green construction.[14]

TABLE 1-6 BENCHMARKS FOR AVERAGE SIZE SINGLE-FAMILY HOMES

	ENERGY STAR for Homes(1)	LEED for Homes	NAHB Model Green Home Building Guidelines	National Green Building Standard
Bedrooms	Square Feet (SF) of Conditioned Area			
1	1,000	900		2,501 to 4,000 SF is point-neutral, regardless of number of bedrooms
2	1,600	1,400	1,382	
3	2,200	1,900	1,890	
4	2,800	2,600	2,648	
5	3,400	2,850	3,424	
6	4,000	Add 250 SF for each additional bedroom		
7	4,600			
8	5,200			

(1) For homes permitted after January 1, 2011.

HOME SIZE ADJUSTMENT FACTOR

The larger a home, the more resources are used to build it and the more energy is consumed to operate it. To account for the environmental impact of home size, rating systems have instituted incentives for building smaller homes. Often, points are awarded for smaller homes and offset for larger homes. Because there is a correlation between home size and the number of bedrooms, the benchmark, or point-neutral home size, is typically expressed in square feet of conditioned area per number of bedrooms, as shown in Table 1-6.

NOTES

1. USGBC, *LEED for Homes Reference Guide*, 2008, p. 2.
2. EPA press release, "EPA Announces ENERGY STAR Homes Reach Nearly 17 Percent Market Share for 2008," July 2, 2009.
3. EPA, "National Awareness of ENERGY STAR for 2008: Analysis of CEE Survey," p. ES-1.
4. These numbers include homes certified during the pilot phase of the program. LEED for Homes officially launched in 2008.
5. Although the Guidelines were published in 2005, the NAHB Research Center did not begin certifying homes until February 2008.
6. EPA Press Release, July 2, 2009.
7. Marie Coleman, Communications Coordinator, USGBC, email to the author, July 16, 2009.
8. Anne Holtz, Director of Communications, NAHB Research Center, email to the author, August 3, 2009.

9. Michelle Desiderio, NAHB Research Center Director of Green Building Programs, email to the author from Anne Holtz, NAHB Research Center, July 28, 2009.

10. "NAHB Model Green Home Building Guidelines," 2006, p. 1.

11. "LEED for Homes Reference Guide," USGBC, 2008, p. 31.

12. "Green Home Building Rating Systems—A Sample Comparison," prepared by NAHB Research Center, Inc., March 2008, p. 11.

13. "LEED AP Candidate Handbook: Valid for July 2009," 2009, Green Buildings Certification Institute, p. 5.

14. www.nahb.org, "Green Building for Building Professionals" course description; accessed October 10, 2009.

2

COMMERCIAL RATING SYSTEMS: A COMPARISON

The three commercial rating systems described in detail in this book were selected because of their acceptance in the building industry and their national scope. Using a rating system provides designers, constructors, and owners with a metric to verify the relative sustainability of their projects. Targeting a level of sustainability using an established rating system can help ensure that initial goals are maintained through construction completion. As a project progresses, budget, schedule, and other pressures can threaten to subvert the best intentions. When attaining a level of certification is an agreed-on priority, sustainable attributes are less likely to fall by the wayside.

This chapter gives a brief overview and comparison of ENERGY STAR® for Buildings and Plants, Green Globes®, and LEED®-NC. More information on each rating system, as well as illustrative case studies, can be found in later chapters.

BRIEF OVERVIEW OF COMMERCIAL SYSTEMS

ENERGY STAR for Buildings and Plants

ENERGY STAR for Buildings and Plants is a voluntary program of the U.S. Environmental Protection Agency (EPA) and the Department of Energy

(DOE), launched in 1995. Ratings are awarded based solely on energy efficiency, although tools that track water use also are available. After one year of operation the energy performance of new or existing buildings is benchmarked against a database of actual energy use by similar buildings. Buildings performing in the top 25 percent for energy efficiency qualify for the ENERGY STAR. Construction documents for buildings designed to meet ENERGY STAR targets may earn the Designed to Earn the ENERGY STAR label, but a year of utility data must be reviewed before the completed building can earn the ENERGY STAR.

Green Globes

Green Globes was originally developed by a private Canadian company using the United Kingdom's BREEAM (BRE Environmental Assessment Method) as a starting point. In 2004, the Oregon-based nonprofit organization Green Building Initiative® (GBI) acquired the license to promote and develop Green Globes in the United States. Points are awarded in a range of categories similar to those listed Table 2-3. Projects are scored as a percentage of points achieved, with points irrelevant to the project deducted from the 1,000 points available prior to calculating the percentage. Project teams purchase an online software subscription and complete a survey for every category at each of the eight stages of design and construction. The software tool tracks project scoring as the project progresses and suggests ways to raise the score. Green Globes has a rating system for new construction and major renovations (NC) and for continuous improvement of existing buildings (CIEB). Both commercial and multifamily residential projects may qualify for certification.

LEED

The LEED (Leadership in Energy in Environmental Design) Green Building Rating System™ was developed by the U.S. Green Building Council (USGBC). The pilot program for what is now LEED for New Construction and Major Renovations (LEED-NC) was launched in 1998. In 2009, the LEED family of rating systems and pilot programs included:

LEED-NC
LEED for Existing Buildings: Operations & Maintenance
LEED for Commercial Interiors
LEED for Core & Shell
LEED for Schools
LEED for Retail

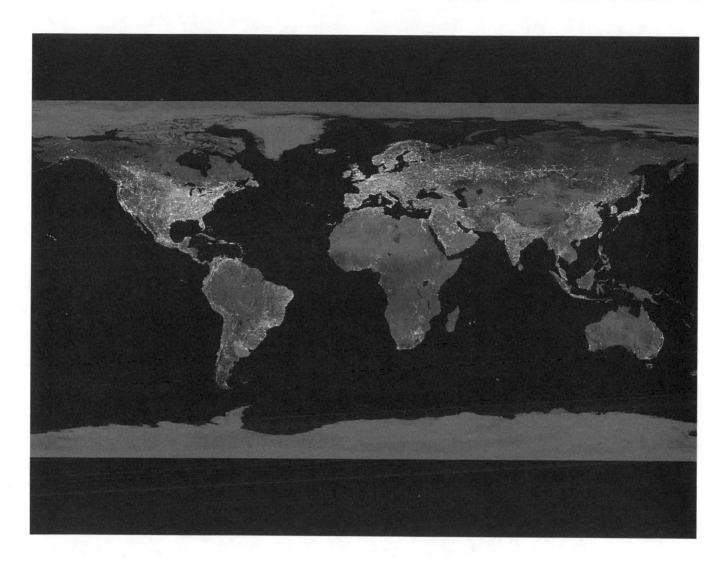

LEED for Healthcare

LEED for Homes

LEED for Neighborhood Development

Figure 2-1 Evidence of light pollution on Earth is visible at night from space. *Image courtesy of NASA/Goddard Space Flight Center Scientific Visualization Studio, http://visibleearth.nasa.gov.*

For LEED-NC, there are up to 110 points available in categories similar to those listed in Table 2-3. LEED also offers an online tool that teams must use to access credit templates, upload project documentation, and track progress.

ELIGIBILITY

Because ENERGY STAR benchmarks a building's actual energy use against an existing database of similar buildings rather than against a computer model of anticipated energy use using a baseline model, only building types for which an adequate database of energy use exists can qualify for the

TABLE 2-1 PROJECT TYPES ELIGIBLE FOR CERTIFICATION

	ENERGY STAR	Green Globes	LEED
Eligible Building Types	Bank/financial institutions, courthouses, hospitals, hotels, K-12 schools, medical offices, religious worship facilities, retail, residence halls/ dormitories, supermarket/ groceries, warehouses, and wastewater treatment plants	Commercial and multifamily residential. Multifamily projects must be four stories or higher.	Commercial over 1,000 SF, or over 250 SF for LEED-CI
New Construction/ Major Renovations	✓	✓	✓
Existing Buildings	✓	✓	✓

ENERGY STAR. There are no such restrictions for Green Globes or LEED (see Table 2-1).

MARKET PENETRATION/BRAND RECOGNITION

Sustainable commercial buildings can offer significant benefits to the environment; to the health and productivity of occupants; and to the owner in the form of lowered operating costs. Having a green building can also give developers an edge in attracting tenants. Certification by a nationally recognized rating system lends credence to claims of greenness, and certification by a recognized brand could contribute to media attention and resulting publicity.

ENERGY STAR is a recognized brand associated with energy efficiency.[1] More than 1 billion square feet of commercial space had earned the ENERGY STAR by the end of 2008.[2] Whereas a design can earn the Designed to Earn the ENERGY STAR label, buildings earn the ENERGY STAR after one year of occupancy, based on actual energy use. As a result, the initial lease-up will be completed without the potential marketing benefit of an ENERGY STAR label. The ENERGY STAR for buildings is awarded for a particular year and must be earned each year based on performance data from utility bills.

Both Green Globes and LEED evaluate sustainable design and construction comprehensively, assessing many aspects besides energy efficiency. LEED is the older and more established rating system and, as shown in Table 2-2, dominates Green Globes in terms of the number of projects certified. A 2008 calculation[3] concluded that LEED-NC certified projects represented 5.8 percent of new construction starts. New LEED-NC registrations were found to represent about 30 percent of the market. LEED-CS

TABLE 2-2 MARKET PENETRATION OF THREE COMMERCIAL ASSESSMENT SYSTEMS

	ENERGY STAR	Green Globes	LEED
Year Launched	1995	2004	1998 (LEED-NC) 2004 (LEED-EB)
Number of Buildings Certified	6,205(1)	30 Green Globes NC(2) 38 Green Globes CIEB(2)	1,870(3) LEED-NC 268(4) LEED-EB
Number of Buildings Registered	N/A	2,300 Green Globes NC and CIEB combined(2)	14,789 LEED-NC(3) 1,406 LEED-EB(4)

(1) As of December 31, 2008.[5]
(2) As of July 22, 2009.[6]
(3) As of July 6, 2009.[7]
(4) As of July 31, 2009.[8]

(LEED for Core & Shell) offers a precertification designation to registered projects to recognize the developer's intent to construct a certified building. This can be a useful marketing tool, but it is not a guarantee of certification.

LEED has clearly established its dominance for comprehensive building assessments in the United States. One Arkansas design professional said, "My general line is that if what you want is a sustainable project, then Green Globes is a good way to keep the project team focused; but if what you want is the project splashed across the newspapers, LEED gets the recognition."[4] Given the length of time it takes to design and construct some commercial projects, Green Globes is a relatively new rating system. There is no way to predict if or how the market might shift as Green Globes matures.

RATING BUILDING PERFORMANCE

Whereas ENERGY STAR assesses only energy use, Green Globes and LEED share similar comprehensive performance targets, as illustrated by Table 2-3. In addition to common categories, each also has two unique categories:

- *Green Globes:* The Project Management category includes an integrated design process, environmental purchasing, and commissioning. It is worth up to 100 out of 1,000 points. The Emissions category, which is worth up to 45 out of 1,000 points, is concerned with minimizing ozone depletion and pollution, and with preventing contamination of waterways and sewers.

- *LEED-NC, LEED-CS, and LEED for Schools:* The Innovation in Design category awards up to 6 points out of a total of 110 for items not covered by LEED, and for exceeding credit requirements. The Regional Priority category offers up to 4 bonus points as incentives to address regional priorities. For example, in regions where water conservation is particularly important, additional points could potentially be earned for exceeding the conservation measures outlined in the Water Efficiency category.

Although Green Globes and LEED share similar performance targets, they take different approaches to incorporating life-cycle analysis (LCA) into their respective rating systems. Green Globes offers an LCA calculator tool to help design teams understand the cradle-to-grave environmental impact of building assemblies. This tool is available free to everyone, and will be incorporated in the Green Globes for New Construction assessment tool in early 2010. As for LEED, in 2004 the USGBC formed a working group to determine how to integrate life-cycle analysis into the system. With the release of LEED 2009, points were weighted to reward LCA-related measures. No LCA calculator or similar measures were incorporated in the LEED rating system, however.

Another difference between the two systems is that LEED has mandatory prerequisites which must be met in order to qualify for certification. Examples include fundamental building commissioning and minimum indoor air quality performance. The intent of these prerequisites is to ensure that specific sustainability goals are met or benefits achieved. Green Globes does not have any mandatory measures, though it does require a minimum number of points be earned in each category.

As the oldest and most well-known comprehensive sustainable rating system, LEED has been subject to criticism over the years. One centered on the lack of greater integration of LCA, which reportedly will be included in future versions of the rating system. Another was that a building did not necessarily have to be energy efficient to receive certification, a flaw that has been addressed in later versions of LEED. To further address the issue of energy efficiency, beginning with projects registered under LEED 2009 (v3), projects receiving certification must commit to providing the USGBC with actual energy and water usage performance data for at least the first five years of occupancy. This will enable the USGBC to compare actual to modeled building performance, provide feedback about operations to owners, and potentially offer useful feedback to design teams.

Another charge against the LEED system was that it could be "gamed," that certification could be attained by pursuing points that were easy to achieve but did not benefit the environment in proportion to the value of a point. In an effort to address this problem, the USGBC increased the total number of points from 69 to 110 and reweighted credits to reflect environmental priorities in LEED 2009.

TABLE 2-3 CATEGORY TYPES CONSIDERED IN RATING BUILDING PERFORMANCE

	ENERGY STAR for Buildings and Plants	Green Globes	LEED-NC
Site Selection and Development		✓	✓
Energy Efficiency	✓	✓	✓
Water Conservation		✓	✓
Material and Resource Efficiency		✓	✓
Indoor Environmental Quality		✓	✓
Additional Categories		Project Management; Emissions	Innovation in Design; Regional Priority

Third-Party Verification

To qualify for certification, third-party review and verification is required for all the rating systems. Verification is as follows:

- *ENERGY STAR:* The ENERGY STAR label, as noted previously, is awarded based on actual energy use reported on utility bills, making verification of design and construction documentation unnecessary. The EPA evaluates reported energy use. To safeguard against energy efficiency coming at the expense of indoor environmental quality, a professional engineer must certify that indoor air pollutants are controlled, adequate ventilation and illumination provided, and thermal conditions met as established by referenced standards.

- *Green Globes:* Two stages of third-party verification are required under Green Globes for new construction.

    - The first stage of assessment occurs at the end of the design phase and consists of a review of construction documents, management records, energy analysis, and other documentation. The assessor checks to see if the percentage of points awarded by the completed questionnaire is supported by the documentation.

    - The second stage of assessment includes further documentation review and a site visit to walk through the building and interview team members. Because of the on-site visit, the GBI says many questions can be resolved and additional documentation requested if required for certification.

- *LEED-NC, LEED-CS, and LEED for Schools:* A review of calculations and documentation is performed in either one or two stages, at the project

Figure 2-2 This parking canopy covered with solar photovoltaic panels produces electricity for the adjacent Adam Joseph Lewis Center for Environmental Studies at Oberlin College, Oberlin, Ohio. *Photo courtesy of Bonnie Yelverton.*

Figure 2-3 Icicles like these on a Maine hotel can form when heat escapes through the roof, melting snow and ice. Water runs off and refreezes at the eave, creating an ice dam that blocks further water runoff. Conditions like this can often be avoided with proper insulation and attic ventilation. *Photo courtesy of National Oceanic and Atmospheric Administration/Department of Commerce.*

team's option. The team can choose a design phase review and construction phase review of documentation for prerequisites and attempted credits, or the team can opt for one final review. The LEED Online tool indicates which credits qualify for design phase review and which for construction phase. It also has a mid-review clarification page that allows the LEED reviewer to contact the team for minor clarifications. Teams may file appeals to contest rejected credits, if any.

EASE OF USE

A potential barrier to using a rating system is the amount of time and effort required to learn about it and implement it. There will, of course, be a learning curve associated with any new rating system, but it may be steeper for some systems and depends in part on a project team's experience. Here are some considerations for each of the systems:

- *ENERGY STAR:* The EPA estimates it takes about six hours to complete the tasks required to submit for the ENERGY STAR, including collecting and inputting data from utility bills and the engineer's time to confirm that the building meets referenced indoor air quality and other standards.[9] From an administrative standpoint, ENERGY STAR for Buildings and Plants is the most time-efficient assessment system; it is, however, also the most limited in scope. Buildings that are Green Globes and LEED certified may also qualify for the ENERGY STAR label. Green Globes has integrated ENERGY STAR's Target Finder tool into its rating system.

- *Green Globes:* The GBI sees its target market as comprising mainstream builders, designers, and developers who are for the most part new to "green."[10] Its online software tool is in the form of a questionnaire, with answers input at each of eight stages of the design and construction process and feedback and suggestions given at each stage. There are no prerequisites and up to 1,000 points are available, giving project teams many options for reaching the desired percentage of credits. One Arizona constructor found the absence of prerequisites in Green Globes to be key: "The main difference [between LEED and Green Globes] is that there are things that if you do them on a project for LEED, it will automatically keep you from getting certification."[11] A project his company constructed earned enough points to become Green Globes certified even though it could not meet a prerequisite required for LEED certification.

The final assessment includes a document review followed by an onsite visit, which includes interviews with project team members. The

TABLE 2-4 POINT SYSTEMS

	ENERGY STAR	Green Globes	LEED-NC
Levels of Certification	1	4	4
Total Points Available	100-point scale	1,000	110
Minimum Points Required for Certification	75 or higher	35% of points applicable to the project	40 points, plus mandatory prerequisites
Point Minimums per Category?	N/A	Yes(1)	No

(1) Anticipated beginning late 2009.

assessor has the opportunity to seek clarification and request additional documentation. After completing the certification process, one architect said, "Green Globes takes a more practical stance than LEED. Its strength is the lack of bureaucracy. It's not easier to qualify but the process is easier."[12]

In terms of becoming practiced with a rating system, one Green Globes rating system is applied to all new construction. In contrast, LEED offers rating systems or has pilot programs for five different rating systems for different new construction commercial building types.

■ *LEED-NC:* 110 points are available, in addition to 8 mandatory prerequisites. Documentation for LEED certification is managed with an online tool available to project team members. Through the tool, responsibilities are assigned and progress is tracked as requirements for prerequisites and attempted credits are completed. Credit templates are supplied, and all documentation is submitted online. Documentation is evaluated either at the end of construction or at the end of both the design and construction phases. There is an established appeals process for attempted credits that are denied; a fee of $500 per contested credit is charged. It is not uncommon for a LEED consultant to be on project teams to give LEED expertise, help establish project goals and integrate sustainable strategies, and provide energy modeling services.

The point systems for the three commercial rating systems are given in Table 2-4.

COSTS OF COMPLIANCE

The administrative costs of ENERGY STAR are low and there are no registration or certification fees. Energy performance is assessed based on a

COMMERCIAL RATING SYSTEMS: A COMPARISON

TABLE 2-5 REGISTRATION AND CERTIFICATION FEES FOR NEW CONSTRUCTION(1)

	ENERGY STAR for Buildings and Plants	Green Globes	LEED
Registration (Members)	$0	Five-Year Software Subscription: $500	$900
Registration (Non-Members)	N/A	Same as above	$1,200
Assessment and Certification (Members)	$0(2)	$7,000 for one building under 100,000 SF up to $15,000 for one building over 500,000 SF	Less than 50,000 SF: $2,250 50,000 to 500,000 SF: $0.045/SF More than 500,000 SF: $22,500
Assessment and Certification (Non-Members)	Same as above	Same as above	Less than 50,000 SF: $2,750 50,000 to 500,000 SF: $0.055/SF More than 500,000 SF: $27,500

(1) Rates are current for 2010. Rates for existing construction can be found in subsequent chapters.

(2) There is no charge for reviewing energy use data submitted from utility bills to demonstrate energy use. A professional engineer must certify that indoor air quality is adequate and this engineer's fee will vary.

year's worth of utility bills. Time costs include gathering the bills and entering the data into an online tool. The other administrative expense is for an engineer's time to confirm the building's compliance with indoor air quality and other referenced standards.

The fixed costs for each rating system are listed in Table 2-5. Many of the additional costs of building for certification are difficult to compare for several reasons. For Green Globes and LEED, these include the different credits that may be selected within each rating system and the variety of projects—in terms of design complexity, size, construction market, and other variables—all of which make a direct cost comparison problematic.

Depending on the options pursued, an energy model, a computer simulation of anticipated energy use based on the building's design, might be required. The cost for this service varies with project size, complexity, and other factors.

Extra construction costs may be incurred for implementing the measures needed to obtain certification, depending on which credits are pursued. In addition, staff may need to spend time learning about the rating system and how to meet requirements for certification; or a consultant might be hired to provide expertise with a particular rating system or with green building in general.

PROFESSIONAL DESIGNATION

Professional designations are available to indicate expertise in or commitment to a rating system, to green building, or both.

- *ENERGY STAR:* ENERGY STAR offers ENERGY STAR Partners, a designation for companies, not individuals. Design firms can seek eligibility for partnership by submitting commercial building designs for new construction that achieve the ENERGY STAR. To be eligible for existing construction partnership, service providers must provide at least 10 benchmarks every 12 months by entering energy data into Portfolio Manager. Partners commit to working with ENERGY STAR to improve the energy performance of commercial buildings. They are listed on the ENERGY STAR website, are permitted to display the ENERGY STAR logo in conformance with the terms in the partnership agreement, and are given access to other ENERGY STAR resources and recognition opportunities. There is no fee for being an ENERGY STAR Partner.

- *Green Globes:* The GBI launched a Green Globes Professional (GGP) designation in 2009 for individuals trained and tested in the Green Globes assessment systems and general green building and operations practices. Candidates for the designation are required to have a minimum of five years' experience in the building industry and some familiarity with sustainable practices. Training and testing are given online and include Life Cycle Assessment, energy modeling, and proficiency with the Green Globes online assessment tools and the certification process.[13] A directory of GGPs will be listed on the GBI website.[14]

- *LEED:* The Green Building Certification Institute (GBCI) is the accrediting body for LEED Accredited Professionals, a designation granted to individuals who pass exams demonstrating expertise with green building and the LEED rating system. Prior to 2009, there was one LEED AP (Accredited Professional) designation. Now candidates take LEED exams in a particular LEED area and receive accreditation in that specialty—for example, a LEED AP-BD+C can be achieved by passing the Building Design and Construction exam that covers LEED-NC. Experience on a LEED project within the past three years is required before taking the credentialing exam. There is also a continuing education requirement for maintaining credentials: 30 hours of approved programs every two years. A directory of LEED APs is posted on the GBCI website. In the Innovation and Design category, one point is awarded for having a LEED AP on the project team.

NOTES

1. In a national consumer survey, 76 percent of households recognized the ENERGY STAR label and 63 percent of households associated the ENERGY STAR label with "efficiency or energy savings," as described in the EPA's "National Awareness of ENERGY STAR for 2008: Analysis of CEE Survey," p. ES-1.

2. "ENERGY STAR Snapshot: Measuring Progress in the Commercial and Industrial Sectors," Spring 2009, p. 1.

3. Rob Watson and Elizabeth Balkan, "Green Building Impact Report 2008," Greener World Media, Inc., 2008, p. 3.

4. Matthew Cabe, Intern Project Architect, Allison Architects, Inc., Fayetteville, Arkansas, telephone conversation with the author, July 14, 2009.

5. "ENERGY STAR Snapshot: Measuring Progress in the Commercial and Industrial Sectors," Spring 2009, p. 6.

6. Mark Rossolo, Director, State and Local Outreach, the Green Building Initiative, email to the author, July 22, 2009.

7. Marie Coleman, Communications Coordinator, the U.S. Green Building Council, email to the author, July 8 and 16, 2009.

8. Ibid., July 31, 2009.

9. Karen Butler, U.S. EPA's manager for ENERGY STAR Commercial New Construction, conversation with the author, July 31, 2008.

10. www.thegbi.org/about-gbi/guiding-principles/position.asp; accessed June 5, 2009.

11. Mike Derkenne, Vice President of Construction Operations for Nelson Phoenix, LLC, telephone conversation with the author, July 29, 2009.

12. Larry Nagaki, LEED AP, Principal at Nagaki Design Build Associates, Inc., Phoenix, Arizona, telephone interview with the author, July 24, 2009.

13. GBI Press Release, "Green Building Initiative Launches Two New Personnel Certification Programs," August 5, 2009.

14. Rossolo, email to the author, June 29, 2009.

3

ENERGY STAR FOR RESIDENTIAL PROJECTS

There are two ENERGY STAR® programs for residential construction: ENERGY STAR for Homes for residential construction three stories and lower, and the pilot program ENERGY STAR for Multifamily High-Rises (MFHR) for most multifamily buildings more than three stories high. The programs are geared primarily toward new construction—although gut renovations may also qualify—and focus on energy efficiency. Third-party verification is required. Both programs are administered by the U.S. Department of Environmental Protection (EPA) and apply only to residences in the United States.

Cost-effectiveness is a core principle of the ENERGY STAR programs, and it is the intent of the EPA that the cost of the requirements for an ENERGY STAR qualified home be offset by the resulting savings in reduced energy costs. The EPA's Cost Effectiveness Policy for the ENERGY STAR for Homes program states, "All program requirements must result in an incremental monthly mortgage cost that is the same or less than the projected monthly savings."[1]

The EPA launched the ENERGY STAR program for single-family homes in 1995 and adopted a revised Version 2 in 2006. To keep up with changes in residential energy efficiency, the EPA has developed Version 3, or ENERGY STAR 2011. It will be required for all homes permitted in the year 2011 or later that seek to earn the ENERGY STAR. Regardless of building permit date, all homes aspiring to qualify for the ENERGY STAR must comply with ENERGY STAR 2011 by July 1, 2011, at the latest.

The information in this chapter on ENERGY STAR 2011 is current as of mid-2009.

ENERGY STAR FOR HOMES

Eligibility

ENERGY STAR for Homes may be earned by any residence three stories or lower in height, whether single-family, multifamily, attached, systems-built, or manufactured. Both new and existing homes are eligible, although an existing home would need to be gutted to expose all exterior framing to meet verification requirements for insulating and air sealing. Third-party verification confirming that the home is constructed to exceed the minimum energy efficiency requirements of the 2004 International Residential Code by at least 15 percent is mandatory. [2] By the end of 2008, ENERGY STAR for Homes had garnered a 17.5 percent market share of the new homes market, and was expecting to reach 20 percent market share, with 1 million ENERGY STAR homes built by the end of 2009.[3]

Note only completed homes are eligible for the ENERGY STAR label; house plans that meet the requirements for energy-efficient construction details and features may receive the Designed to Earn the ENERGY STAR label.

The Process

The process for earning an ENERGY STAR label begins with a plan review by a qualified Home Energy Rater. The home may be evaluated either via the performance path, whereby the rater uses a software model to verify the home meets the energy target, or the prescriptive path, whereby the designer and builder follow a prescribed set of construction specifications. If the set of construction documents meets the minimum requirements, the drawings are eligible to receive the Designed to Earn the ENERGY STAR label.

For a home to earn the ENERGY STAR, the rater must perform construction inspections and performance testing to verify that the home qualifies. Homes that meet the requirements can earn the ENERGY STAR.

Criteria for Earning the ENERGY STAR for Homes

The ENERGY STAR for Homes program emphasizes energy-efficient features in its qualified homes. These include:

- Effective insulation, inspected to ensure proper installation
- High-performance windows

- Tight construction of the building envelope
- Sealed ductwork
- Efficient heating and cooling equipment
- Efficient products such as ENERGY STAR qualified appliances, lighting, and hot water heaters
- Third-party verification to confirm energy-efficient measures are properly installed and performing as expected

Beginning in 2011, the following additional measures will be required:[4]

- Reduced thermal flow, with new requirements for proper insulation installation, reduced thermal bridging, and increased duct insulation
- Reduced airflow, through pressure-balancing and sealing sheetrock at top plates
- Required whole-house mechanical ventilation; spot local exhaust; and water-managed roofs, walls, and foundations.

Home Size Adjustment Factor

ENERGY STAR 2011 will introduce a home size adjustment factor. The EPA has established benchmark home sizes ranging from 1,000 square feet of conditioned floor area for a one-bedroom to 5,200 square feet of conditioned floor area for an eight-bedroom home. Homes larger than the benchmark will require additional energy-efficiency measures to qualify for the ENERGY STAR. The intent is to reduce the carbon footprint of a larger home to that of an average-size home. Refer back to Table 1-6 in Chapter 1 for a list of benchmark home sizes for one to eight bedrooms.

Pathways to Compliance

There are two approaches to earning the ENERGY STAR for Homes: the performance path and the prescriptive path. In either case, third-party verification is required for plan review, construction inspections, and performance testing. Both the performance and the prescriptive paths feature variations for climate based on the climate zones defined in the 2004 International Residential Code, Table N1101.2.

Performance Path

In the performance path, a Home Energy Rater analyzes the construction drawings and specifications and creates a computer model to verify that the expected energy use of the home will meet program requirements. Homes are rated for energy efficiency on a 100-point HERS (Home Energy Rating Standards) Index. The reference home is built to the minimum requirements of the 2006 International Energy Conservation Code (IECC) and has an

Index score of 100. An Index score of zero would be achieved by a net-zero energy home which generates as much energy as it uses.

A minimum score of 85 is required to earn the ENERGY STAR for Homes label. Each 1 percent increase in energy efficiency above the requirements of the IECC corresponds to a 1 percent decrease in the HERS Index; the lower the index score, the more efficient the home. The energy evaluated in the rating comprises that used for heating, cooling, water heating, lighting, appliances, and on-site power generation. On-site power generation cannot be used to lower a HERS Index to meet the ENERGY STAR requirement—that is, there is no trade-off of a base level of energy efficiency for on-site generation.

For Homes Permitted after 2010

Beginning in 2011, the fixed HERS Index will be replaced with a Simulated Performance Method to determine a unique HERS Index Target threshold for each home. The HERS Index Target will be established using ENERGY STAR Reference Design specifications (amended to include state energy code elements, if they exceed ENERGY STAR requirements) and HERS software evaluations. Although renewable energy systems cannot be used to meet the base value of the Reference Design HERS Index, renewable energy systems may be used to meet any additional energy-efficiency requirements resulting from the size adjustment factor.

Prescriptive Path

For Homes Permitted before 2011

In the prescriptive path, a Builder Option Package (BOP) of program-related construction specifications must be met for the home to earn the ENERGY STAR label. The specifications have been crafted and evaluated to ensure that a home built to the prescriptive specifications will meet the level of energy efficiency required to earn the ENERGY STAR for Homes. There is a national BOP and, until 2011, climate-specific ones for Hawaii, California, and the Pacific Northwest.

For Homes Permitted after 2010

Beginning in 2011, the prescriptive path will be an option only for homes that do not exceed the ENERGY STAR benchmark home size. Similar to the national BOP, it is referred to as the ENERGY STAR Reference Design.

ENERGY STAR 2011 requires that any state energy code requirements that exceed the national ENERGY STAR Reference Design Home be incorporated into a regional or state Reference Design Home.[5] This change helps negate the need for separate regional packages and ensures that ENERGY STAR guidelines exceed code requirements. Separate requirements for Hawaii will remain in place owing to the state's unique climate.

Figure 3-1 When a home qualifies for the ENERGY STAR, this label is filled in and typically affixed to the home's electrical panel. *Image courtesy of the U.S. EPA ENERGY STAR Program.*

Third-Party Verification

Field verification by a certified Home Energy Rater is required for homes to qualify for the ENERGY STAR label. There is a Thermal Bypass Checklist inspection to verify air barrier and insulation placement and installation to eliminate the movement of heat around or through insulation. Beginning in 2011, the following inspection checklists, in addition to the Thermal Bypass Checklist, will be field-verified by the rater:

■ The Framing Quality Checklist, to reduce thermal breaks owing to framing conditions.

■ For HVAC Quality Installation, there are separate checklists for the contractor and third-party verifier, with inspections of right-sizing, air distribution, refrigerant charge, and duct installation.

- The Indoor Air Quality checklist covers ventilation, combustion pollutants, and filtration.
- The Water-Managed Construction checklist is used to verify design and construction, manages moisture in the foundation, wall and roof assemblies, and building materials.

Home Energy Raters and BOP Inspectors must be active ENERGY STAR Partners accredited by the RESNET (Residential Energy Services Network) Mortgage Industry National Home Energy Rating Standards or other approved verification oversight organization. They must follow RESNET standards and protocols for testing and verifying the items described in "Criteria for Earning the ENERGY STAR for HOMES," above.

Home Energy Raters can earn accreditation from RESNET as a Sampling Provider, allowing them to qualify a group of multifamily and production homes based on their preconstruction analysis of the building plans and random inspections and testing of a sample set of homes in the field. Sampling, which is an option for both the prescriptive and performance paths, can reduce verification costs for the builder while maintaining quality control. In multifamily buildings, each unit may earn the ENERGY STAR for Homes, but not the building as a whole.

Designed to Earn the ENERGY STAR

From its inception in 1995 through 2008, ENERGY STAR for Homes partnered with more than 6,000 builders to produce more than 940,000 ENERGY STAR homes. The program makes specifications available and requires a local rater or BOP Inspector to review plans before construction begins. In 2008, the EPA introduced the Designed to Earn the ENERGY STAR program for homes, under which construction documents may be awarded a Designed to Earn the ENERGY STAR label to display on the drawings. Previously, because the great majority of homes built in the United States are not custom homes, the ENERGY STAR for Homes program focused exclusively on homebuilders.

The qualification process begins with a Rater or BOP Inspector evaluating the drawings and specifications using either the performance path, which includes energy modeling, or the prescriptive path for consistency with the BOP specifications. Designs that meet the requirements of ENERGY STAR will receive a Designed to Earn the ENERGY STAR label for the documents. Designers seeking to have their drawings awarded the Designed to Earn label must be ENERGY STAR for Homes Partners.

DESIGNED TO EARN THE ENERGY STAR

This home plan meets strict energy efficiency guidelines set by U.S. EPA. Field verification is required for the home to earn the ENERGY STAR label.

www.energystar.gov

Figure 3-2 This logo may be displayed on the construction documents of designs meeting the ENERGY STAR for Homes guidelines. *Image courtesy of the U.S. EPA ENERGY STAR Program.*

A Designed to Earn label (see Figure 3-2) on drawings does not automatically result in an ENERGY STAR Home. The verification and testing procedures required for a home to earn the ENERGY STAR are the same regardless of whether or not the design has been awarded the Designed to Earn the ENERGY STAR.

ENERGY STAR Partners

Builders, developers, and designers are among the building professionals who are eligible to become ENERGY STAR Partners. Partners are listed in a database on the ENERGY STAR website that is searchable by profession and state. Free technical and marketing support and recognition programs are also available to Partners. To remain active Partners, builders and designers must meet ENERGY STAR guidelines for at least one home per year. For their part, developers must commit to qualifying all homes in their community for the ENERGY STAR. All partners must agree to terms of use regarding the ENERGY STAR logo.

Indoor airPLUS

Beginning in 2011, ventilation, combustion pollutant control, and filtration measures specified in the EPA's Indoor airPLUS Verification Checklist will be a mandatory part of the ENERGY STAR for Homes requirements. Until then, ENERGY STAR qualified homes that comply with the EPA's Indoor airPLUS specifications and verification requirements may receive the ENERGY STAR Indoor airPLUS label. The label, which complements the ENERGY STAR for Homes program, may not be earned by a home that is not an ENERGY STAR home.

Indoor airPLUS is intended to improve indoor air quality by verifying such measures as moisture control, radon control, pest barriers, HVAC system features, combustion systems and garage isolation, building materials, and home commissioning.

Figure 3-3 Compliance with the EPA's Indoor airPLUS program is optional in ENERGY STAR qualified homes until 2011. *Image courtesy the U.S. EPA Indoor Environments Division.*

ENERGY STAR for Homes and Other Rating Systems

A prerequisite for the LEED for Homes Energy & Atmosphere Credit 1 is meeting the performance requirements of ENERGY STAR for Homes, including third-party verification. Additional points are awarded for exceeding these performance requirements. The ENERGY STAR Indoor Air Package (now Indoor airPLUS) is also a pathway in the Indoor Environmental Quality category.

For the National Green Building Standard, homes that qualify for the ENERGY STAR achieve the bronze level for the Energy Efficiency category without pursuing any other credits in the category.

Figure 3-4 Situated in a retirement community, this home is accessible to wheelchair users. *Photo by Isaac Zuercher.*

Climate: Mixed-Humid (Zone 4)

Size: 1,793 square feet conditioned space, plus a 240-square-foot unconditioned sunroom; two bedrooms, two-and-a-half baths

Completion Date: 2006

Construction Cost: About $380,000

HERS Index Score: 73

Builder: Zurich Homes, Crossville, Tennessee

Designer: Ted Zilius Design, Morrisville, Vermont

Rater: Home Energy Concepts, McMinnville, Tennessee

HVAC Contractor: Action Heating and Cooling, Crossville, Tennessee

This custom home was built in the Uplands retirement village for owners who were relocating from northern Vermont. Accustomed to cold winters and anticipating hot summers, the owners recognized that an energy-efficient home could save energy costs and help the environment. "The Tennessee home is much more comfortable than the other two homes we have lived in," co-owner

Sidney Nichols said.[6] The home is also wheelchair-accessible to comply with the development's requirements.

Figure 3-5 South-facing windows are shaded by deciduous trees in the summer, allowing for solar heat gain in the winter. *Photo by Isaac Zuercher.*

Energy-Efficient Features

Construction followed the performance path and met ENERGY STAR requirements for duct sealing, a tight building envelope, and other requirements. Walls were framed with 2 × 6 lumber to provide space for additional insulation. Windows on the north side are minimal while those on the south side are large. Large oak trees on the south side of the home were preserved to lend summer shading. Solar tubes bring daylight into several interior rooms.

Tips from the Builder

Isaac Zuercher, co-owner of Zurich Homes, said, "We found that two key components are quality insulators and HVAC contractors. Also, the Home Rater should be willing to meet with you before you start construction and review your design and the standards that are required."[7]

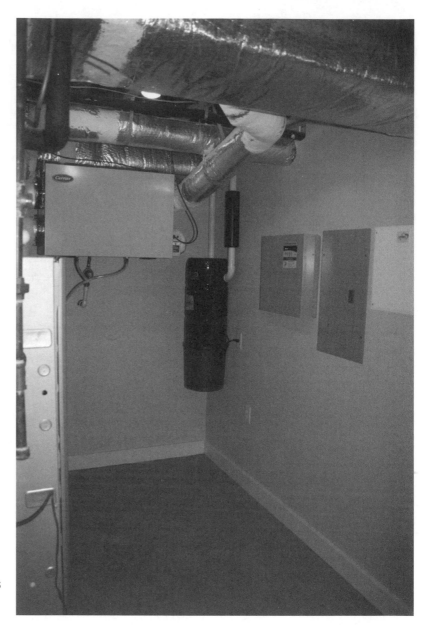

Figure 3-6 The mechanical room features insulated and sealed ductwork, a 13.0 SEER air conditioner, a natural gas hot water heater, and a 94.1 AFUE furnace. *Photo by Isaac Zuercher.*

Tips from the Owner

"Plan on spending more in construction costs; know yourself (by conducting research) what additional steps are needed to make it ENERGY STAR rated; and make sure your contractor knows what it takes to make [your home] ENERGY STAR rated," said Nichols.[8]

Clayton i-house
Prefabricated Home

▲ **Figure 3-7** The roof of the one-bedroom unit (left) accommodates rainwater harvesting; the flex room (right) is shown with a roof deck. *Image courtesy of Clayton Homes.*

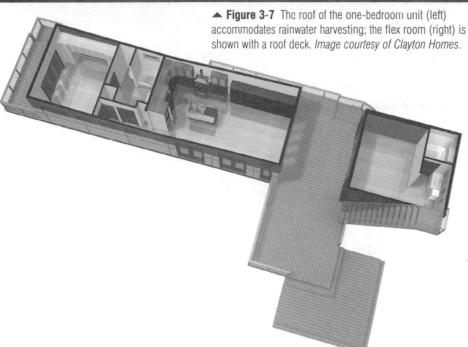

◀ **Figure 3-8** Decks, made with recycled-content materials, extend off the master bedroom and connect the main house with the flex room. *Image courtesy of Clayton Homes.*

Climate: Varies.

Size and Base Cost: One bedroom, one bath, 723 square feet: $74,900. Two bedrooms, one bath, 1,023 square feet: $93,300. Flex room addition with one bath: from 268 square feet and $26,660.

HERS Index Score: Varies. Homes are "ENERGY STAR ready" and need to be certified in their installed location.[9] Foundation type, climate, and other factors will affect the score.

Designer and Fabricator: Clayton Homes, Maryville, Tennessee

Figure 3-9 The master bedroom features bamboo flooring, an ENERGY STAR ceiling fan, and generous natural daylight and ventilation. *Image courtesy of Clayton Homes.*

Energy-Efficient and Sustainable Features

Energy-efficient features include energy-efficient windows, compact fluorescent lighting, ENERGY STAR appliances, and formaldehyde-free fiberglass insulation. Walls have R-21 insulation; ceilings and floors have R-30 insulation. Other sustainable features include dual-flush toilets and low-flow faucets, a rainwater catchment system, and no-VOC paint. Solar panels, a tankless water heater, and bamboo flooring are options. Exterior materials are durable, with fiber-cement board siding and standing seam metal roof.

Comments from the Fabricator

Clayton Homes built and sold 31,700 homes in 2008 and expected to build and sell 28,000 in 2009. About 30 percent of the company's homes are built to ENERGY STAR criteria and go on to earn the ENERGY STAR in the field. Says Chris Nicely, vice president of marketing at Clayton Homes, "Anytime you can affiliate yourself with a great icon like ENERGY STAR, you will benefit. I can't point to a single sale that was finalized because of the ENERGY STAR affiliation, but I do know that the story behind the i-house is stronger as a result."[10]

Figure 3-10 This home is one of 326 ENERGY STAR qualified homes in an over-55 community. "We really felt like it was the 'right thing to do' to help our country's energy crisis, to lower our homeowner's energy cost outlay, and to, hopefully, encourage sales," said Ted Nissly of the McKee Group. *Photo courtesy of the McKee Group.*

Climate: Mixed-Humid (Zone 4)

Size: 1,224 to 2,000 square feet, two bedrooms and two baths. There are 326 units of 10 different models in this over-55 community of ENERGY STAR homes.

Completion Date: 2007

Sale Price: $199,990 to $366,900

HERS Index Scores: Range from 76 to 84, with an average of 78. Houses are also certified at the bronze level of the National Green Building Standard.

Builder: The McKee Group, Springfield, Pennsylvania

Designer: Grimaldi Architecture, Horsham, Pennsylvania

HERS Rater: EIC Inc./Comfort Home, Lancaster, Pennsylvania

HVAC Engineer: EIC Inc./Comfort Home, Lancaster, Pennsylvania

Energy Sealing/Infiltration Control: EIC Inc./Comfort Home, Lancaster, Pennsylvania

Figure 3-11 ENERGY STAR appliances are among the energy-saving features of this home. *Photo courtesy of the McKee Group.*

Energy-Efficient Features

Energy-efficient features include ENERGY STAR low-e argon-filled windows; R-38 attic insulation; 92 percent high-efficiency, direct vent heaters; and an HVAC system designed to ACCA Manual J (heat gain/loss), Manual D (duct sizing), and Manual S (equipment sizing) specifications. Ducts were sealed with mastic. The air infiltration package included caulking, foaming, and sealing the building envelope.

Tips from Builder

Ted Nissly of the McKee Group says, "It's important for the builder to put the correct team together at the very beginning, including the architect, the HERS rater, the HVAC system designer, the insulation contractor, and the construction manager. The builder must learn enough to have a general working knowledge of the process but needs to look to the experts for their particular areas of expertise. Find a third-party HERS rater who is service-oriented, cost-conscious, and 'builder friendly,' and involve the whole team from the conception of the project."[11]

Regarding any additional costs for earning an ENERGY STAR label, Nissly said, "There is an up-front one-time cost of about $800 to have the required HVAC design done, and a recurring cost of about $700 per house to have the required energy sealing work done, along with the required testing, documentation and verification. In our case, it only cost another $250 per house to be verified as meeting the NAHB Green Standards. We did not need to upgrade any specifications beyond those required to meet ENERGY STAR."[12]

ENERGY STAR FOR MULTIFAMILY HIGH-RISES PILOT PROGRAM

The EPA's pilot program for the ENERGY STAR for Multifamily High-Rises (MFHR) applies primarily to new construction. It was launched in 2006 with projects in New York and Oregon, and was later expanded to Colorado, Georgia, New Jersey, Texas, and Nevada in order to gather data from different climates.

In undertaking the pilot program, the EPA identified four challenges in the MFHR building type that could not be addressed by the existing ENERGY STAR programs for homes or commercial buildings:[13]

- There is a split incentive in multifamily high-rise buildings, in that the costs of improving energy efficiency are paid by the developer or owner, but the resulting savings typically go to the tenants.
- Tenant turnover in MFHR is high, making tenant education difficult. Occupant behavior and building management can have a significant impact on energy use.
- Current residential modeling tools do not accurately model energy consumption in multifamily high-rise buildings.
- Benchmarking the energy consumption of new projects to similar building types, as done in the ENERGY STAR program for commercial buildings, is difficult because there is very little data publicly available on comparable buildings.

At the time this book was being written, the pilot phase of the MFHR program was still under way, so the EPA had not yet determined the feasibility of establishing a national ENERGY STAR program for multifamily high-rises; nor had it identified what, if any, changes would be made as a result of the pilot if the program were to be launched nationally.

The EPA's agreement with pilot partners cited the following criteria as those it would use to determine whether the ENERGY STAR MFHR pilot program would be extended nationally:[14]

■ The performance specifications must be cost-effective.

■ The program must represent true energy savings over standard construction.

■ The program must provide value in the marketplace to MFHR stakeholders.

■ The program must be easy to implement and understand, including energy modeling and verification protocols.

Eligibility and Criteria for Earning the ENERGY STAR for MFHR

The pilot program applies to new construction of multifamily buildings four stories or higher. To be eligible for the ENERGY STAR label, the performance target of pilot projects must exceed by at least 20 percent the minimum requirements for energy efficiency in ASHRAE 90.1 2004, Appendix G. Projects must also be modeled to obtain a score of 75 or better on the EPA's MFHR benchmark tool, indicating performance in the top 25 percent of similar buildings nationally. Benchmarking is based on information on comparable buildings collected by the Residential Energy Consumption Survey (RECS) of home energy use and costs, conducted by the Energy Information Administration of the U.S. Department of Energy.

Also in progress are quality assurance measures such as reviews of energy modeling and inspections of construction. Buildings, not individual units, may earn the ENERGY STAR under this pilot program.

Figure 3-12 Intervale Green was built on a long-vacant site once visited by President Jimmy Carter to bring attention to urban decay. A few years later, the shoot-out scene in the movie *Fort Apache, the Bronx* was filmed there. Located only half a block from a subway station, the building is convenient to public transportation. *Photo courtesy of WHEDCo.*

Climate: Mixed-Humid (Zone 4)

Space Type: Multifamily residential with ground floor commercial

Size: 128 units (one to three bedrooms each); 140,801 square feet residential, 6,800 square feet commercial

Completion Date: 2008

Construction Cost: $155 per square foot

Total Development Costs: $39,237,815

Owner/Developer: Women's Housing and Economic Development Corporation (WHEDCo), Bronx, New York

Architect: Edelman, Sultan, Knox, Wood/Architects LLP, New York, New York

Energy Consultant: Steven Winter Associates, Inc., New York, New York

Structural Engineer: Robert Silman Associates, New York, New York

Mechanical, Electrical, and Plumbing Engineer: Abraham Joselow, P.C., P.E., New York, New York

General Contractor: Mega Contracting, Inc., Astoria, Queens

Figure 3-13 The project has 20,000 square feet of green roof, some of it accessible to residents. Residents also have access to two private courtyards and a public sculpture garden featuring the work of local Bronx artists. *Photo courtesy of WHEDCo.*

Figure 3-14 Fluorescent lighting and occupancy sensors in common areas help reduce the building's energy load. *Photo courtesy of WHEDCo.*

Energy-Efficiency Costs and Savings

Energy-efficient costs and savings were as follows:[15]

Estimated hard costs associated with energy reduction measures: $437,750

Projected total energy (all fuels) costs saved annually: $82,492 (over baseline ASHRAE 90.1 2004 building)

Simple payback period: 5.3 years

Savings-to-investment ratio: 2.8

Incentives and green building support were provided by Enterprise Green Communities, NYSERDA Multifamily Performance Program, Bronx Overall Economic Development Corporation's Bronx Initiative for Energy and the Environment, Home Depot Foundation, New York City Council, and the Bronx borough president.

This multifamily residential project was developed on a triangle of city-owned property that had been vacant for more than 25 years. All apartments are rented to people earning below 60 percent of the area median income. "We pursued the ENERGY STAR designation to set an example that high-rise green building can be both affordable and beautiful," said WHEDCo president Nancy Biberman.[16] The project includes two green roofs totaling 20,000 square feet, a private backyard, an entry courtyard, and a public garden.

Energy-Saving Features

The building is expected to use 33.4 percent less energy than the ASHRAE 90.1 2004 baseline building, resulting in projected savings of 208,401 kWh electricity and 3,410 MMBtu annually. Energy-saving features consist of a high-performance building envelope, which includes air sealing, continuous insulation, and insulated low-e argon-filled windows; 85 percent efficient boilers and hot water heaters; carbon monoxide sensors in the garage, so ventilation only runs when needed; and ENERGY STAR lighting fixtures and appliances. The design team also received a code modification to reduce the excessive ventilation rate to a lower level while maintaining good air quality. Cary Trochesset, project manager for Edelman, Sultan, Knox, Wood/Architects LLP, said that without the ventilation waiver it would have been difficult to earn the ENERGY STAR.[17] The New York City building code has since been updated to make ventilation waivers unnecessary.

In addition to the two green roofs, part of which are accessible to tenants, green features include recycled-content flooring; low-flow faucets and shower-heads; and low-VOC paints, adhesives, and sealants.

Tips from the Developer

Nancy Biberman of WHEDCo offers the following tips when undertaking ENERGY STAR for multifamily high-rise projects:

- "Familiarize the entire design and development team with ENERGY STAR goals. Green features can too easily become an afterthought in the face of a major construction project. Every party on the design and development team should know the ENERGY STAR checklist for a given project, and should be made aware of which measures are nonnegotiable and tied to project funding.
- "Engage the energy consultant as part of the development team, early and often. The architects, engineers, and contractors should get to know the energy consultants and use them as a resource, and the consultants should keep a close eye on construction progress, from beginning to completion.
- "Ensure the construction lender understands the funding mechanism and anticipates incentive disbursements. While the ENERGY STAR program is fairly simple, lenders should be made aware prior to implementation."[18]

Tips from the Architect

Randy Wood, AIA, principal at Edelman Sultan Knox Wood/Architects LLP said his firm had already been incorporating many of the energy-efficient practices required by the ENERGY STAR MFHR pilot program into the firm's projects. "I don't consider myself an expert; I just think it's what we should be doing, and we're doing it," said Wood. "If there was anything that I found difficult, it was getting contractors to understand what they had to do and getting them to do it." Woods gave as an example sealing ductwork to comply with the specifications, rather than as the subcontractor was accustomed to doing—which did not pass performance testing.[19]

Edelman Sultan Knox Wood designs many low-income and subsidized multifamily high-rises and Wood says that now many clients are asking them to evaluate the feasibility of participating in the ENERGY STAR program.[20]

RESOURCES

ENERGY STAR, www.energystar.gov/homes: Here you will find links to the following resources for new homes: technical guidelines for designing and constructing an ENERGY STAR home, including the Thermal Bypass Checklist; national and regional Builders Option Package specifications; information and resources on ENERGY STAR for affordable homes; listings of builders and designers that are ENERGY STAR Partners; and information on becoming a Partner.

Residential Energy Services Network, www.natresnet.org: This website has information on, and tells how to locate, Home Energy Raters and Building Option Package Inspectors. Or visit the ENERGY STAR website (above).

NOTES

1. "ENERGY STAR Qualified Homes 2011 Fact Sheet," revised May 4, 2009, p. 4.
2. The 2004 International Residential Code is the reference for ENERGY STAR, but the RESNET reference for the HERS rating is the 2006 International Energy Conservation Code.
3. Sam Rashkin, National Director, ENERGY STAR for Homes, telephone conversation with the author, February 19, 2009.
4. "ENERGY STAR Qualified Homes 2011 Fact Sheet," pp. 1–2.
5. EPA, "ENERGY STAR 2011 Frequently Asked Questions," revised April 28, 2009.
6. Sidney Nichols, email to the author, February 20, 2009.
7. Isaac Zuercher, co-owner of Zurich Homes, email to the author, February 13, 2009.
8. Nichols, email to the author, February 20, 2009.
9. Brandon O'Connor, Clayton i-house, email to the author, forwarded by Justin Kidd, Retail Marketing, Clayton Homes, July 8, 2009.
10. Justin Kidd, Clayton Homes, email to the author, July 13, 2009.
11. Ted Nissly, CGP, CGB, Product Development, the McKee Group, email to the author, February 25, 2009.
12. Ibid.

13. "ENERGY STAR Pilot Project Agreement For Multifamily High-Rise Pilot Partners (Draft)," undated, sent to the author by Ted Leopkey, Program Analyst, ENERGY STAR Residential Branch, August 22, 2008.

14. Ibid.

15. In email attachment sent by Debbie Grunbaum, Director of Communications and Development at WHEDCo, to the author on June 19, 2009.

16. Ibid.

17. Cary Trochesset, Project Manager, Edelman, Sultan, Knox, Wood/Architects LLP, telephone conversation with the author, July 8, 2009.

18. In email attachment sent by Debbie Grunbaum, Director of Communications and Development at WHEDCo, to the author on June 19, 2009.

19. Randy Wood, telephone conversation with the author, June 29, 2009.

20. Ibid.

4

LEED FOR HOMES

LEED® for Homes is a national rating system developed by the nonprofit U.S. Green Building Council (USGBC) and launched in 2008. Up to 136 points may be earned in eight different categories: Innovation and Design Process; Location and Linkages; Sustainable Sites; Water Efficiency; Energy and Atmosphere; Materials and Resources; Indoor Environmental Quality; and Awareness and Education. There are four different levels of certification: Certified (45 to 59 points), Silver (60 to 74 points), Gold (75 to 89 points), and Platinum (90 to 136 points). Points required may vary owing to the Home Size Adjustment described later in this chapter.

ELIGIBILITY

LEED for Homes may be applied to new and gut-rehab residential projects including single-family detached, attached, and multifamily buildings up to three stories. To participate, each unit must have its own cooking and bathroom facilities. A gut-rehab must be substantial; it must include replacing HVAC equipment, windows, and other systems and components, and must open exterior walls for inspection. Every unit in a multifamily building must be certified, and at the same level—that is, buildings cannot be partially certified. Modular and manufactured homes can be certified only after they are constructed on site. Mixed-use projects may qualify if at least 50 percent of the space is residential.[1] A pilot program for multifamily buildings four to six stories is underway and will run through 2010.

To be eligible for LEED for Homes certification, the project must be registered with the USGBC; meet the 18 prerequisites; meet or exceed category point floors in four categories (Sustainable Sites, Water Efficiency, Materials & Resources, and Environmental Quality); and achieve a minimum overall score, which depends on level of certification sought and home size. Documentation that credits have been met and third-party verification by a Green Rater are also required. As of mid-2009, only homes located in the United States, U.S. territories and military bases, and Canada may participate.[2]

THE PROCESS

The USGBC describes the process for participating in LEED for Homes in five steps:[3]

1. The builder or project manager selects a LEED for Homes Provider (more information on Providers and Green Raters can be found under "Third-Party Verification," below).

2. The builder establishes a project team, which identifies sustainability goals and strategies for meeting them; the Provider or Green Rater evaluates the design and estimates the score and certification level achievable.

3. The home is built; it is inspected by the Green Rater during construction (typically, just before drywall is installed) and after construction is completed.

4. After performing the final inspection and performance tests, the Green Rater submits project documents to the LEED for Homes Provider for review and submission to the USGBC for certification.

5. The builder sells the home. The USGBC makes available marketing materials related to LEED certification, which the builder can use in promoting the sale.

THE COST

The cost for registering a single-family house for LEED for Homes in 2009 was $150 for USGBC members and $225 for nonmembers; certifying fees were $225 for members and $300 for nonmembers. For multifamily housing, the registration fee was $450 for members and $600 for nonmembers, and the certification fee was $0.035 per square foot for members and $0.045 per square foot for nonmembers.

Another LEED for Homes project cost is the fees for the Green Rater and HERS rater. Fees are set by individual raters and vary based on the project scope, certification level sought, the builder's expertise in sustainable construction, project location, and other factors.

Additional potential costs include those for implementing some of the prerequisites and optional credits, and the time to document credits, which will vary by project and project team. As with any rating system, there will likely be a learning curve while project team members familiarize themselves with LEED for Homes and its requirements. The *LEED for Homes Reference Guide*, a necessary resource, is available from the USGBC for $100 for members and $125 for nonmembers.

The cost increment will vary according to the level of sustainability of the homes the builder is accustomed to building, project team experience, and other factors. The USGBC reports single-family homes that were certified at a cost premium of $500 or less.[4]

THIRD-PARTY VERIFICATION

Verification of some prerequisites and points by an approved third party is required for LEED for Homes certification as a quality assurance measure. In other cases, the builder is responsible for inspection, or provides calculations to the Green Rater for review; or a tradesperson must sign an accountability form indicating that a requirement has been met.

The USGBC contracts with, trains, and supports LEED for Home Providers—42 in the United States and Canada in 2009. Providers are responsible for finding, training, and auditing Green Raters according to USGBC guidelines.[5] Providers contract with Green Raters throughout their region to work directly with builders to provide support on sustainable design and construction, inspect construction, and review documentation.

When multiple units of the same model home are built by the same contractors, a sampling protocol may be used in place of inspections of every unit. In that case, one out of three units would be inspected in the builder's first LEED for Homes subdivision, one out of five in the builder's second subdivision, and one out of seven for builders who have constructed three or more LEED for Homes subdivisions.

HOME SIZE ADJUSTMENT

As the size of a home grows, so does the amount of materials used and energy consumed. The USGBC suggests that "as home size doubles, energy consumption increases by roughly one-quarter, and material consumption increases by roughly one-half."[6] To account for the impact of home size and the fact that there is a correlation between the number of bedrooms and the number of occupants, LEED for Homes adjusts the number of points required for certification based on the number of bedrooms and total square feet of the home. The threshold required for each level of certification may be adjusted by either additional points (up to 10) for larger homes with proportionally fewer bedrooms, or reduced by up to 10 points for smaller homes with proportionally more bedrooms. The USGBC's *LEED for Homes Reference Guide* contains a chart for calculating the adjustment for single-family homes. A spreadsheet is also available with the online checklist for calculating the adjustment for multifamily projects. For the purposes of determining the threshold adjustment, the term "bedroom" includes any room that meets fire and building code requirements for a sleeping room and could be used as a bedroom, even if it is not labeled as such on the house plans.

CERTIFICATION CRITERIA FOR HOMES THREE STORIES OR FEWER

The LEED for Homes project checklist of available credits is divided into eight categories with a total of 136 optional points, as well as 18 mandatory items known as prerequisites. The USGBC has a "LEED for Homes Rating System" document available for free download from its website. The 100-plus page document includes the checklist and describes the credits, including intent, prerequisites, and synergies and trade-offs with other available LEED for Homes credits. It is a useful document to refer to when considering whether to pursue certification with LEED for Homes. The more extensive *LEED for Homes Reference Guide* also includes information on environmental issues the credits are designed to address; suggested approaches for doing so; documentation needed and the party responsible for documentation; verification requirements; and resources. The *Reference Guide* is available for purchase.

The following overview of the LEED for Homes rating system is summarized by category from the *LEED for Homes Reference Guide*.[7]

Innovation and Design Process

This category covers integrated project planning, durability management, and innovative or regional design. Up to 11 points are available. Under the "Innovative or Regional Design" heading, up to four credits may be created by submitting written strategies or approaches not covered in the rest of the LEED for Homes rating systems, including exceeding the requirements of some credits. Innovative Design Requests must include the specific requirements for the proposed credit, documentation for compliance, and the expected impact. The Provider submits proposed credits to the USGBC for approval.[8]

Innovation and Design Prerequisites

- *Integrated Project Planning: Preliminary Rating.* The builder, rater, and other key project team members must meet "as early as practical" to determine the level of certification to target, to identify the credits to meet to achieve the targeted level, and to identify the team member responsible for each credit selected.

- *Durability Management Process: Durability Planning.* Before construction, the project team must evaluate and plan for (by incorporating measures in the drawings and specifications) all potential moderate and high risks to durability, including moisture control and site- and climate-specific issues. The Project Checklist on the USGBC website includes a Durability Risk Evaluation Form, and the *Reference Guide* contains a table of indoor moisture control measures.

- *Durability Management Process: Durability Management.* The durability measures required in the previous prerequisite will be managed and inspected by the builder during construction. A point can be earned by having independent third-party verification. The Project Checklist document contains a template that may be used to document inspections.

Location and Linkages

This category focuses on the location of the site, rewarding development near existing infrastructure, such as utilities and public transportation, and within walking distance to amenities, like restaurants, retail stores, and libraries. There are no prerequisites, and there is no minimum number of points required in this category.

There are two pathways for earning credits, both of which can earn up to 10 points. The first is to comply with the LEED for Neighborhood Development rating system, a separate LEED rating system that addresses the environmental responsibility of a development's location and overall design. The alternate pathway is to comply with prescriptive requirements, such as avoiding environmentally sensitive sites, building in or near existing communities, building in or near existing infrastructure, building in locations that minimize dependency on cars, and providing access to open space.

Sustainable Sites

This category addresses the design of the site selected for development. Up to 22 points are available. Credits are given for minimizing site disturbance, taking sustainable landscaping measures, reducing heat island effects, managing surface water, controlling pests by nontoxic means, and implementing compact development.

Sustainable Sites Prerequisites and Point Minimum

- *Site Stewardship: Erosion Control during Construction.* Plan and implement erosion control measures, including stockpiling disturbed topsoil for reuse; controlling runoff; and protecting on-site lakes, streams, and storm sewer inlets.

- *Landscaping:* Introduce no invasive plants.

- *Point Floor:* A minimum of 5 points of a possible 22 points must be achieved in the Sustainable Sites category.

Water Efficiency

This category focuses on water conservation in terms of water reuse (rainwater harvesting, graywater systems, and municipal recycled water systems), irrigation systems (both increasing efficiency and decreasing demand), and reducing indoor water use. There are no prerequisites for Water Efficiency, but a minimum of 3 out of 15 possible points must be achieved.

There's No Accounting for Occupants

How occupants live in a home can have a huge impact on its performance, but in most cases a home receives certification prior to occupancy, regardless of the rating system used. Therefore, rating systems tend to be largely occupant-neutral, taking into account the lifespan of the home instead of the series of people who may live in it. The Awareness and Education prerequisite in LEED for Homes requires that owners receive training and education in operating and maintaining the home's LEED features and equipment, with the intent that the home's performance be maintained. However, while a sustainable home can be designed and constructed, only the people who occupy it can control how it is operated.

One example of the impact occupants can have on performance is illustrated in the first LEED for Homes Platinum project, certified during the pilot phase of the rating system. It was designed and constructed as a net-zero energy home in Edmond, Oklahoma, by Ideal Homes of Norman, Oklahoma (see Figures 4-1 and 4-2). After-occupancy performance monitoring found energy consumption exceeded modeled predictions. By setting the air conditioning at 70 degrees instead of 76 degrees, it is estimated that the occupants used two-and-a-half times more cooling energy.[9]

Figure 4-1 South-facing solar photovoltaic panels generate energy while the roof overhang provides some relief from the summer sun. *Photo courtesy of Ideal Homes, www.Ideal-Homes.com.*

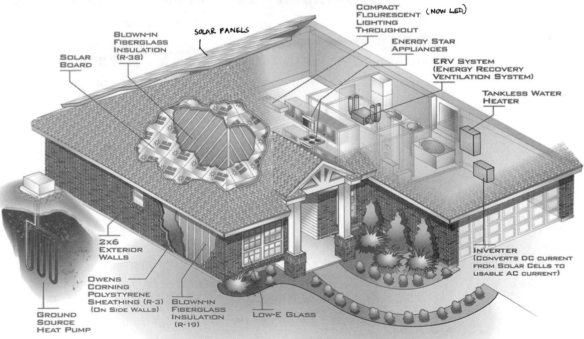

COMPACT
FLOURESCENT (NOW LED)
LIGHTING
THROUGHOUT

ENERGY STAR
APPLIANCES

ERV SYSTEM
(ENERGY RECOVERY
VENTILATION SYSTEM)

TANKLESS WATER
HEATER

BLOWN-IN
FIBERGLASS
INSULATION
(R-38)

SOLAR PANELS

SOLAR
BOARD

2x6
EXTERIOR
WALLS

OWENS
CORNING
POLYSTYRENE
SHEATHING (R-3)
(ON SIDE WALLS)

BLOWN-IN
FIBERGLASS
INSULATION
(R-19)

LOW-E GLASS

INVERTER
(CONVERTS DC CURRENT
FROM SOLAR CELLS TO
USABLE AC CURRENT)

GROUND
SOURCE
HEAT PUMP

Figure 4-2 A tight well-insulated building envelope and efficient equipment, combined with a ground source heat pump and solar panels, helped move this home toward net-zero energy use over the course of a year. *Image courtesy of Ideal Homes, www.Ideal-Homes.com.*

Energy and Atmosphere

Users choose to follow one of two pathways, either performance or prescriptive, both of which can earn up to 38 points. The performance pathway uses energy modeling software to estimate the design's energy performance. The alternate path does not require energy modeling, instead prescribing specific measures such as a tight, well-insulated building envelope and efficient mechanical equipment. A prerequisite for both pathways is to test any air conditioning system to ensure proper refrigerant charge.

Energy and Atmosphere Performance Path

The prerequisite for the performance path is to meet the energy performance requirements of ENERGY STAR for Homes, described in the previous chapter. Points are earned for exceeding ENERGY STAR requirements, with a maximum of 34 points for a net-zero energy home. Additional points may be earned for efficient hot water distribution and pipe insulation.

Energy and Atmosphere Prescriptive Path

The prerequisites for the prescriptive path include basic insulation, reduced envelope leakage, good windows, reduced heating and cooling distribution losses, good HVAC design and installation, and ENERGY STAR lights. In each case, points can be earned by exceeding the requirements of the prerequisites. Additional points may be earned by measures such as efficient water heating and appliances.

Materials and Resources

Points are awarded in three areas: material-efficient framing (including detailed framing documents and prefabricated systems); environmentally preferable products, which have recycled content, low-emissions, and/or are produced within 500 miles of the project site; and reduced construction waste.

Materials and Resources Prerequisites and Point Minimum

- *Material-Efficient Framing: Framing Order Waste Factor Limit.* The overall waste factor for framing orders must not exceed 10 percent. The waste factor may be calculated in board feet or by cost.

- *Environmentally Preferable Products: FSC-Certified Tropical Wood.* Builders must state a preference for FSC-certified hardwoods to their wood product suppliers and request information on the country of manufacture for products supplied and a list of FSC-certified products available. If tropical woods are required in the project, they must be FSC-certified or reclaimed.

- *Waste Management: Construction Waste Management Program.* Builders must explore and document recycling and other waste diversion options available locally, and document the diversion rate of project waste.

- *Point Floor.* A minimum of two points in this category is required.

Indoor Environmental Quality

There are two pathways to choose from in the Indoor Environmental Quality category: the performance path and the prescriptive path. The performance path requires compliance with ENERGY STAR for Homes indoor air quality measures, which is described in Chapter 3. Additional points may be earned by exceeding these requirements. The alternate path requires prescriptive measures such as moisture control, outdoor air ventilation, local exhaust, distribution of space heating and cooling, air filtering, contaminant control, radon protection, and garage pollutant protection. A minimum of six points in this category must be achieved.

Indoor Environmental Quality Performance Path

Thirteen points may be earned by meeting the EPA Indoor airPLUS requirements. (This program is referred to in the *Reference Guide* as the ENERGY STAR Indoor Air Package, but was subsequently renamed by the EPA.) Additional LEED points in other categories (such as Innovation and Design, for durability measures) may be available. Energy and Atmosphere prerequisite 6.1 for a good HVAC design and installation is complementary to Indoor airPLUS. Additional points may be earned, with eligible optional prescriptive path measures improving performance above Indoor airPLUS requirements.

Meeting the requirements of the EPA Indoor airPLUS program earns LEED credits, but if an ENERGY STAR label is also sought, then requirements are more extensive. For ENERGY STAR, the Indoor airPLUS label may only be earned by an ENERGY STAR qualified home. Beginning in 2011, the indoor air requirement will be mandatory for earning the ENERGY STAR.

Indoor Environmental Quality Prescriptive Path

The prerequisites for the prescriptive path include basic combustion venting measures, outdoor air ventilation, local exhaust, room-by-room load calculations, good filters, radon-resistant construction in homes in EPA Radon Zone 1, and no HVAC system components in the garage. Additional points can be achieved by exceeding the requirements of the prerequisites and by controlling contaminants during and after construction.

Awareness and Education

The prerequisite for Awareness and Education is the first requirement addressing the occupant's behavior. Operating and maintenance manuals, as well as documentation and education relating to the credits earned for LEED for Homes certification, must be turned over to the owner. A walk-through for the purpose of educating the owner or tenant in the use and maintenance of equipment is required. Additional points may be earned by exceeding the requirements of the prerequisite.

LEED FOR HOMES AND ENERGY STAR

LEED for Homes uses the ENERGY STAR for Homes program as pathways in two categories: Energy and Atmosphere and Indoor Environmental Quality. The alternate pathway in Energy and Atmosphere references ENERGY STAR labeled products, including windows, programmable thermostats, lights, and appliances. It also cites some ENERGY STAR performance criteria for HVAC equipment and skylights.

Figure 4-3 Downspouts direct rainwater from the roof into two 1,700-gallon underground cisterns. The water is used in the drip irrigation system during the drier months. Timer controls activate watering zones in the drought-tolerant landscaping beds. *Photo by Jennifer Hopkins, courtesy of Mark L. Hixson Design-Build.*

Climate: Cold (Zone 5)

Size: 3,045 square-foot conditioned space; 1,173-square-foot garage and unfinished storage; four bedrooms, four-and-a-half baths

Construction Cost: $453,000

Completion Date: 2007

Designer/Builder: Mark L. Hixson Design-Build, Boise, Idaho

Green Rater: OnPoint Advantage LLC, Hidden Springs, Idaho

Mechanical Contractor: Heating Equipment Co., Caldwell, Idaho

Insulation Contractor: Marv's Insulation, Meridian, Idaho

Plumbing Contractor: DeBest Plumbing, Boise, Idaho

Points Achieved: 79.5, Gold

Boise, Idaho, Custom Home Points Achieved (Gold Certification)	
Innovation & Design	8
Locations & Linkages	9
Sustainable Sites	17
Water Efficiency	7
Energy & Atmosphere	14
Materials & Resources	13.5
Indoor Environmental Quality	9
Awareness & Education	2

Sustainable Features

This home's energy performance is expected to be as much as 50 percent better than required by code. Energy-efficient measures include a 95 percent efficient variable-speed furnace with fresh air ventilation and MERV 16 filter (for low-particulate, cleaner indoor air); a 15 SEER air conditioning unit using R410A Freon; ENERGY STAR qualified appliances, lights, windows, and space conditioning equipment; and air-locked entry vestibules. Ducts are sealed and air infiltration minimized per ENERGY STAR requirements in the Energy and Atmosphere performance path. The home earned an ENERGY STAR label with the Builder Option Package.

Water-efficient features include rainwater harvesting (see Figure 4-3) to feed a drip irrigation system and drought-tolerant landscaping. Advanced framing techniques reduced the amount of lumber needed. All lumber waste was recycled, and more than 50 percent of all construction waste was diverted from landfills. Sustainable materials include locally processed concrete, roof material, wall framing, sheathing, floor joists, and trusses. Low-VOC primer and paint, composite decking with recycled content, Green Label carpet and pad, and FSC-certified wood doors were used. Sidewalk concrete that was headed for landfills was recycled in the retaining walls and as masonry veneer (see Figure 4-4).

Figure 4-4 Recycled concrete was diverted from landfills and used for retaining walls and as a masonry veneer. *Photo by Jennifer Hopkins, courtesy of Mark L. Hixson Design-Build.*

Mark L. Hixson Design-Build estimated the additional costs of pursuing LEED certification as follows: registration and certification fees to the USGBC, approximately $250; LEED Rater consultant fee and ENERGY STAR test fees, $4,000; additional staff time for research, documentation, and planning meetings with vendors and subcontractors, approximately $2,000; and a subscription to BuildingGreen.com and purchase of the *Greenspec Directory*, about $300.

Tips from the Builder

"The knowledge and ability to integrate practical construction methodology with innovative new products and technologies is crucial. Don't try to do it all. Choose the things that will make the most impact for your area and scope of project and do them well. Document everything."[10]

Comments from the Homeowner

"I didn't think building a green-built home would be affordable, but the utility bills are no different than our previous 1,400-square-foot home. Having a LEED home, with savings on power, water, and gas—it's just amazing to us, and allowed us to move into a nicer, bigger house." The owner said he worked closely with the builder to look at trade-offs and determine the most cost-effective LEED points to pursue.[11]

CASE STUDY 2

Villa Trieste Production Homes, Las Vegas, Nevada

Figure 4-5 The Venezia model is one of four models offered in the Villa Trieste community. All homes have roof-integrated solar systems. Centralized battery storage is provided at the substation level to store excess energy for use when needed. *Photo © 2009, Pulte Homes and the Communities of Del Webb.*

Climate: Hot-Dry (Zone 3)

Project Type: 185 production homes: four models, five floor plans

Size: Two or three bedrooms, two-and-a-half baths; 1,497 to 1,777 square feet

Completion Date: 2009

Builder/Developer: Pulte Homes, Las Vegas, Nevada

Provider: Sonoran LEED for Homes LLC

Points Achieved: 90, Platinum

Villa Trieste, Las Vegas, Nevada Points Achieved (Platinum Certification)	
Innovation & Design	7.5
Locations & Linkages	7
Sustainable Sites	17.5
Water Efficiency	7
Energy & Atmosphere	25
Materials & Resources	11
Indoor Environmental Quality	13
Awareness & Education	2

Pulte Homes pursued a LEED rating at Villa Trieste because it saw LEED as the best and most recognized third-party certification program in the market. The project also followed the Southern Nevada Home Builders Association Green Built Standards and the Environments for Living Green Certified Program, a turnkey service for builders. "We have been very pleased with the early sales numbers; and traffic for Villa Trieste has been almost two times greater than competitor communities in the same area," said Walter Cuculic, director of strategic marketing for Pulte Homes. "The homes at Villa Trieste are priced at a premium over competitor communities. The premium is due to a combination of the solar, LEED certification, energy efficiency, modern floor plans, and eco-Concierge Dashboard."[12]

Figure 4-6 Every home has an ecoConcierge unit, which tracks the home's energy use and offers comparisons to average use in the community. *Image © 2009, In2 Networks, Inc. In2 Solar Dashboard, www.in2networks.com.*

Figure 4-7 This park area and a community pool are available to residents. *Photo © 2009, Pulte Homes and the Communities of Del Webb.*

The U.S. Department of Energy provided $7 million to the University of Nevada–Las Vegas's Center for Energy Research, in partnership with Pulte Homes and NV Energy, to develop this demonstration community so as to reduce peak residential energy demands. It is expected that these homes will be more than 60 percent more efficient than the 2006 International Energy Conservation Code.

Sustainable Features

The 185 homes in the community have roof-integrated solar-electric power systems. Excess power from these systems is stored in a centralized battery substation until needed. Each home has a "dashboard" monitor that displays current energy use and generation (see Figure 4-6). The dashboard also compares the home's use to that of the average home in the community.

The mechanical system includes 15 SEER air conditioning units and 92 percent efficient furnaces. Other sustainable features include tankless hot water heaters, local materials, products made with recycled content, and ENERGY STAR lights and appliances.

Tips from the Builder

"Talk with several LEED for Home Providers. Each LEED for Home Provider offers very different levels of service."[13]

Figure 4-8 This was the first LEED-certified home built by Lakeland Habitat for Humanity. The keys were presented to the homeowner at this dedication event. *Photo courtesy of Lakeland Habitat for Humanity.*

Climate: Hot-Humid (Zone 2)

Project Type: Affordable single-family home

Size: 1,041 square feet conditioned space, 1,192 square feet total; three bedrooms, one-and-a-half baths

Completion Date: 2008

Construction Cost: $58,294

Builder/Developer: Lakeland Habitat for Humanity, Lakeland, Florida

Designer: Garey Sanford Design Center, Inc., Lakeland, Florida

Green Rater: Florida Solar Energy Center, Cocoa, Florida

Mechanical Contractor: Simpson Air Conditioning, Lakeland, Florida

Electrical Contractor: Southern Power Solutions, Lakeland, Florida

Plumbing Contractor: Sparkman Plumbing, Lakeland, Florida

Pest Control: Bruce Pest Control, Lakeland, Florida

Points Achieved: 54, Silver

Lakeland, Florida Affordable Home Points Achieved (Silver Certification)	
Innovation & Design	3
Locations & Linkages	10
Sustainable Sites	8
Water Efficiency	4
Energy & Atmosphere	11
Materials & Resources	8
Indoor Environmental Quality	10
Awareness & Education	0

Sustainable Features

Part of Lakeland Habitat for Humanity's mission is to make homes as inexpensive to live in as possible. The organization has been building ENERGY STAR Homes for years and saw LEED as a possible way to further decrease the homeowner's costs. While the building design was not modified from a design used for other non-LEED certified homes, its mechanical system was. This home includes a 14 SEER air conditioner for greater energy efficiency and a MERV 8 filter for better air quality.

Cost savings were realized in both soil and landscaping material by clearing the site only for the building footprint, preserving existing grass, and landscaping around existing vegetation. Paperless gypsum wallboard was used in all wet areas to reduce the risk of mold. To minimize construction waste and improve the acoustical barrier between bedrooms and common areas, scrap gypsum wallboard was cut up and used to fill in the space between studs. Many of these strategies used to achieve LEED certification have become standard practice for all homes constructed by this Habitat for Humanity chapter.[14]

The construction cost was several thousand dollars less than that for a similar house nearby that was not in the LEED for Homes pilot program; this savings does not reflect the extra time Habitat for Humanity's team leader spent on the LEED for Homes project. Habitat was not required to pay for LEED registration and certification, and the services of the Provider were also donated.

Although Lakeland Habitat for Humanity received donations of time and labor, some features they would have liked to have included (such as tankless hot water heaters, a graywater reuse system, ultra-low flow plumbing fixtures, solar power, and spray foam insulation) were beyond the reach of the organization.[15]

Tips from the Builder

Habitat's team leader Kim French suggests, "Start earlier. Take the time to do the design charrette. A builder or developer committed to LEED for all their projects needs suppliers and subs who will work with them. Two books that I've found helpful are *Building Green for Dummies* and *Building an Affordable House* by Fernando Pages Ruiz."[16]

LEED FOR HOMES MID-RISE PILOT PROGRAM

The Mid-Rise Buildings Pilot Program covers buildings of four to six stories with at least two units. In this program, the whole building is certified, not individual units, and common areas and mixed-use areas are included in the certification requirements and for calculating fees.[17] The mid-rise pilot program uses the same number of prerequisites, point totals per category, and point totals overall as the LEED for Homes program. A four-page addendum to the LEED for Homes system for the pilot program lists 17 changes to specific credits or prerequisites. These changes are intended to tailor the system to mid-rise buildings in terms of referenced codes and standards, value, and relevance.[18] The USGBC expects to incorporate the mid-rise program in its next *LEED for Homes Reference Guide*.[19]

CASE STUDY 4

Multi-Family Mid-Rise, Pearl Place, Portland, Maine

Figure 4-9 The five-story building (left) was certified Silver under the LEED for Homes Mid-Rise Buildings Pilot Program, while the three-story building on the right was certified Gold under LEED for Homes. *Photo courtesy of Avesta Housing.*

Climate: Cold (Zone 6)

Size: 36,000 square feet in five-story mid-rise building; 36 units: 14 one-bedroom, 13 two-bedroom, and 9 three-bedroom units

Completion Date: 2008

Construction Cost: $8.72 million

Net Development Cost: $11.9 million

Owner: Avesta Housing, Portland, Maine

Architect: Winton Scott Architects, Portland, Maine

Landscape Architect: Carroll Associates, Portland, Maine

Civil Engineer: Gorrill-Palmer Civil Consultants, Gray, Maine

Mechanical/Plumbing Engineers: Mechanical Systems Engineers, Yarmouth, Maine

Electrical Engineer: Bartlett Design, Bath, Maine

Structural Engineer: Becker Structural Engineers, Portland, Maine

Builder: Ledgewood Construction, South Portland, Maine

LEED Consultant: Fore Solutions, Portland, Maine

Points Achieved: 68.5, Silver

Pearl Place, Portland, Maine, Mid-Rise Pilot Points Achieved (Silver Certification)	
Innovation & Design	7
Locations & Linkages	10
Sustainable Sites	14
Water Efficiency	7
Energy & Atmosphere	11
Materials & Resources	6.5
Indoor Environmental Quality	11
Awareness & Education	2

The Pearl Place project consists of two adjacent buildings, a 3-story building with 24 units and a 5-story building with 36 units, built on a site previously occupied by a light industrial warehouse and parking lots. The two buildings are similar in construction and received the same number of points in every category except Energy and Atmosphere, in which the mid-rise building received six fewer points. "The energy scores are different because of the different energy

Figure 4-10 The owner provides heat, hot water, and high-speed Internet access to the units and all utilities for common areas. Tenants are responsible for electricity. *Photo courtesy of Avesta Housing.*

modeling protocols [the Mid-Rise Pilot uses ASHRAE 90.1] and the way USGBC converts the modeling score to LEED points," explained LEED consultant Jennifer Huggins of Fore Solutions.[20] Huggins added that the USGBC is discussing ways to alter the ASHRAE 90.1 baseline to better fit mid-rise residential projects.

The Pearl Place mid-rise building is projected to save almost 20 percent more energy than the ASHRAE 90.1 baseline building and to garner nearly 18 percent cost savings in energy. The building earned the ENERGY STAR.

Sustainable Features

Energy-efficient performance at Pearl Place is achieved in part with a well-insulated building envelope. For example, the exterior walls consist of 2 × 6 studs with interior horizontal 1 × 3 furring; the cavity was filled with dense-pack cellulose insulation; and joints and gaps were tightly sealed. Other energy-efficient features include the heating and ventilation systems, including full air-to-air ventilation with a heat recovery system and programmable thermostats; all appliances and light fixtures are ENERGY STAR; and there are daylight sensors in the stairwells and motion sensors in the corridors. Other sustainable features include many durable and recyclable materials, locally purchased framing lumber and concrete, zero- or low-VOC paints, and Green Label Plus carpeting. All plumbing fixtures are water-efficient, and a rigorous construction waste management plan resulted in an average of 95 percent of waste diverted from

Figure 4-11 Pearl Place was built on a site previously developed with a warehouse building, which was demolished. *Photo courtesy of Avesta Housing.*

the landfill. Pearl Place is located downtown within walking distance of public transportation, shops, and other amenities.

Tips from the Developer

"If you are going to pursue LEED certification, make the commitment as early in the planning process as possible, and employ a comprehensive integrated design approach," advises Development Officer Ethan Boxer-Macomber of Avesta Housing. "Many residents seem to generally value and appreciate the various benefits of living in a green building—physical comfort, indoor air quality, and a general sense that their home was designed and built to be as environmentally friendly as possible. Not only has this helped us market the units to prospective residents, but it has also helped Avesta to advocate for affordable housing in the region." [21]

Boxer-Macomber sees the LEED for Homes Mid-Rise Pilot program as a useful green architecture benchmark for multifamily residential projects, with good name recognition for the LEED brand. However, he suggests LEED for Homes 2008 could better account for geographic differences and go further in ranking urban development over greenfield or auto-dependent suburban development.

Tips from the Architect

Pandika Pleqi, LEED AP, associate at Winton Scott Architects, said, "Having the rating process more streamlined and simplified compared to LEED-NC, and therefore less costly, is a good step toward making this [LEED for Homes pilot] more accessible and appealing to housing project developers. Typically, these projects come with a very strict budget." [22]

Tips from the Builder

Clint Gendreau, project manager at Ledgewood Construction, says, "The higher the LEED certification you are going for is typically proportional to the paper-work needed. It's important to know before the project starts what the LEED expectations are. If you can provide the LEED criteria during the submittal phase, there is minimal cost impact . . . other than the addition of an assistant project manager [a part-time position estimated to have added about $20,000 to this project].

"There are a handful of tips and red flags that I'm sure most contractors are aware of. Dark-colored low-VOC paint is difficult to cover with just two finish coats. Water-based adhesives cause a punchlist headache. Energy-efficient light is changing every day, so what you submit today, may not be compliant when time for install. Drywall manufacturers have different quantities in recycled content from plant to plant." [23]

RESOURCES

USGBC *LEED for Homes Reference Guide*: This is an essential reference for project team members. Less comprehensive information on LEED for Homes can be downloaded for free from the USGBC website, www.usgbc.org.

NOTES

1. Matthew Libby, Manager, Residential Alliances, USGBC, and Nate Kredich, Vice President, Residential Development, USGBC, email to the author, February 23, 2009.

2. USGBC, "Scope and Eligibility Guidelines for LEED for Homes Projects: 2008 Version," May 22, 2009, p. 3.

3. *LEED for Homes Reference Guide,* U.S. Green Building Council, 2008, pp. 5–7.

4. Libby and Kredich email, February 23, 2009.

5. The USGBC/GBCI is scheduled to release a comprehensive uniform Green Rater training program in late 2009, per Matthew Libby, Manager, Residential Alliances, USGBC, and Nate Kredich, Vice President, Residential Development, USGBC; email to the author, February 23, 2009.

6. *LEED for Homes Reference Guide*, p. 9.

7. Information is summarized from the USGBC's *LEED for Homes Reference Guide,* 2008.

8. It is likely that the USGBC will align and coordinate LEED for Homes credits with other LEED rating systems, as was done with a group of other LEED rating systems in LEED 2009. This change would probably take place in late 2010 or 2011, per Matthew Libby, and Nate Kredich email to the author, February 23, 2009.

9. Robert Hendron, Ed Hancock, Greg Barker, and Paul Reeves, "Field Evaluation of a Near-Zero Energy Home in Oklahoma." Proceedings of ES 2007 Energy Sustainability 2007, Long Beach, California, June 27–30, 2007, p. 10.

10. Pati King, Mark L. Hixson Design-Build, email to the author, February 3, 2009.

11. Micheal Seabolt, telephone conversation with the author, February 17, 2009.

12. Walter Cuculic, Director of Strategic Marketing, Pulte Homes, email to the author, February 26, 2009.

13. Ibid.

14. Kim French, Team Leader, Habitat for Humanity of Lakeland, email to the author, February 21, 2009.

15. Ibid.

16. Ibid.

17. Matthew Libby and Nate Kredich email, February 23, 2009.

18. Building Knowledge, Inc., "Summary of Changes to LEED for Homes for Mid-Rise Buildings," June 15, 2008.

19. Matthew Libby and Nate Kredich email, February 23, 2009.

20. Jennifer Huggins, LEED AP, Assistant Project Manager for Fore Solutions, email to the author, February 5, 2009.

21. Ethan Boxer-Macomber, email to the author, May 28, 2009.

22. Pandika Pleqi, LEED AP, Associate, Winton Scott Architects, email to the author, June 15, 2009.

23. Clint Gendreau, Project Manager, Ledgewood Construction, email to the author, February 20, 2009.

5

NAHB MODEL GREEN HOME BUILDING GUIDELINES

The NAHB (National Association of Home Builders), a trade association with the mission of enhancing the climate for housing and the building industry,[1] developed the voluntary *NAHB Model Green Home Building Guidelines* (NAHB Guidelines) for the mainstream homebuilder[2] in 2005. The NAHB Guidelines focus on seven categories, or "guiding principles": Lot Design, Preparation, and Development; Resource Efficiency; Energy Efficiency; Water Efficiency; Indoor Environmental Quality; Operation, Maintenance, and Homeowner Education; and Global Impact. Guidelines for Site Planning and Development are given in the appendix of the document, but no points are awarded in this category.

The NAHB Guidelines allow builders to rate new single-family homes at three levels: bronze, silver, and gold. A minimum number of points in each category is required at each level, plus 100 additional points from any categories at every level (see Table 5-1). Many project-specific variables affect the number of points required and available, but roughly 237 points are required for bronze, 311 for silver, and 395 for gold. Again, depending on the project, total points available range anywhere from approximately 582 to 867.

The NAHB National Green Building Program™ (NAHB Green), launched in 2008, features an online Green Scoring Tool, green building

TABLE 5-1 POINTS REQUIRED FOR THREE LEVELS OF GREEN BUILDING

	Bronze	Silver	Gold
Lot Design, Preparation, and Development	8	10	12
Resource Efficiency	44	60	77
Energy Efficiency*	37	62	100
Water Efficiency	6	13	19
Indoor Environmental Quality	32	54	72
Operation, Maintenance, and Homeowner Education	7	7	9
Global Impact	3	5	6
Additional Points from Sections of Your Choice	100	100	100

*If the home does not have a ducted distribution system for space heating and cooling, deduct 15 points from the number required in the Energy Efficiency section.

Source: *NAHB Model Green Home Building Guidelines* (Washington, DC: National Association of Home Builders, 2006), p. 7. © 2006, National Association of Home Builders. Reproduced with permission.

educational resources, and a green home certification program that supports the NAHB Guidelines. The NAHB Research Center, a subsidiary of the NAHB, accredits verifiers and administers the certification program.

ELIGIBILITY

The NAHB Guidelines were designed to be used for construction of new single-family homes. There are no project registration requirements. To receive certification, homes must be verified to have earned the required number of points by an NAHB Research Center accredited verifier.

Although builder focused, design is an important element of the NAHB Guidelines. The "underlying ideas" for building a green home are, first, that the project's impact on the environment needs to be considered from the start of design, and, second, that the house must be looked at holistically when selecting which guideline items to include in the project.[3]

The NAHB Guidelines are also intended to be used as a "toolkit" for local homebuilding associations to use to create or expand regional green building programs.[4] The points in the national NAHB Guidelines are weighted according to the climate in Baltimore, Maryland (Zone 4).

THE PROCESS

A copy of the *NAHB Model Green Home Building Guidelines*, including a checklist for scoring and a user's guide, can be downloaded at no charge from the NAHB Green website. The steps for receiving green certification using the NAHB Guidelines are as follows:[5]

1. The designer or builder enters project information on NAHB Green's online Green Scoring Tool. The tool (available for free use following registration at www.nahbgreen.org) takes users through the checklist of items that can receive points. In addition to a checkbox for claiming points for each item, there are links to additional information on how to verify the item, its intent, how to implement it, and additional resources. As the user moves through the checklist, a scorecard that tracks the anticipated points in the category is displayed, along with the total points required for each level of certification. The completed checklist, or Designer's Report, can then be exported and downloaded as an Excel spreadsheet.

2. At the start of construction, the builder selects an NAHB accredited verifier, forwards the Designer's Report to the verifier, and schedules a rough inspection with the verifier. The verifier notifies the NAHB Research Center that the rough inspection is scheduled. This marks the point at which the home enters the certification process.

3. At the conclusion of the rough inspection, the verifier sends the report to the NAHB Research Center for review. The Research Center will send the builder a Program Participation Agreement, unless an agreement with the builder is already on file from a previous project.

4. The builder pays the NAHB Research Center the green building certification fee and returns the Program Participation Agreement to the NAHB Research Center, along with proof of insurance.

5. After the verifier performs the final inspection, the final Verification Report is signed by the verifier and builder and submitted to the NAHB Research Center. The Research Center reviews the report and issues the Certified Green Home certificate to the builder.

Figure 5-1 illustrates the steps toward certification.

THE COST

The costs in 2009 for certifying a building with the *NAHB Model Green Home Building Guidelines* were $200 for NAHB members and $500 for nonmembers. Verifier fees are set by individual verifiers and vary based on the project size, systems complexity, whether the builder requested consulting services during design and planning, and other factors. In 2008, the NAHB Research Center estimated plan review and verification costs at $750 per home for up to 10 homes, dropping to $350 per home for builders constructing more than 500 homes per year.[6]

Additional potential costs include implementing green building practices, and the time to enter information into the Green Scoring Tool and

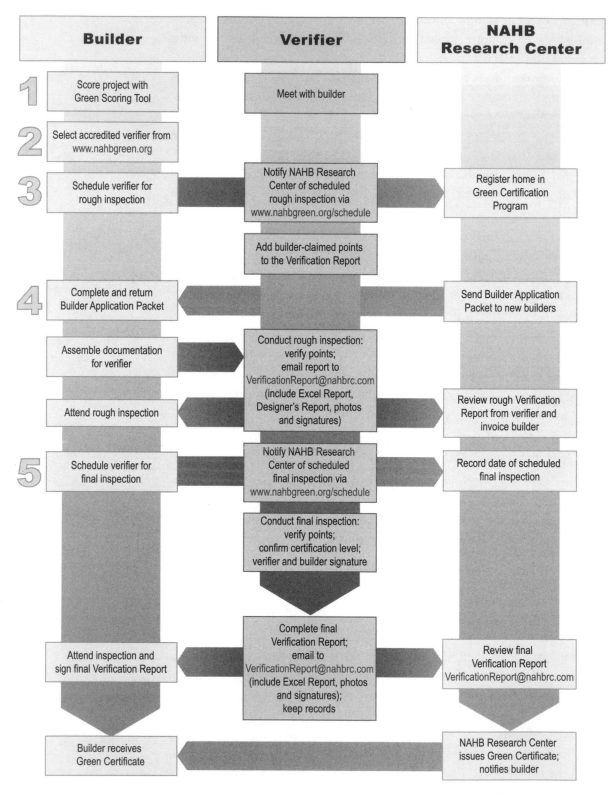

© 2009 NAHB Research Center

Figure 5-1 Flowchart of the certification process for the *NAHB Model Green Home Building Guidelines* and the National Green Building Standard. *Courtesy of NAHB Research Center, http://nahbgreen.org/Content/pdf/cert_flowchart.pdf.*

document credits, which will vary by project and project team. As with any rating system, there will likely be a learning curve while project team members familiarize themselves with the *NAHB Model Green Home Building Guidelines* and its requirements.

THIRD-PARTY VERIFICATION

Verification by a third party is required to confirm that the builder has met the intent of the items selected from the checklist. A list of NAHB-accredited verifiers is available on the NAHB Green website. As of mid-2009, there were 339 verifiers in 48 states with the number steadily growing.[7]

Verifiers review documentation and make two site visits to confirm compliance with the NAHB Guidelines. A rough inspection is performed before drywall is installed and after framing and insulation are complete and building systems are roughed in; a final inspection is conducted after construction is substantially complete but before the closing. In some cases, a builder may produce adequate documentation, such as verification by another third party, for the points sought, precluding the need for a rough inspection by a NAHB-accredited verifier.[8]

At the conclusion of each inspection, the builder and verifier sign the verifier's checklist, after which the verifier submits it to the NAHB Research Center for review and processing.

HOME SIZE

To encourage the efficient use of materials and resources, points are awarded to homes that are smaller than average based on the number of bedrooms. Similar in intent to the LEED for Homes home size adjustment, these credits are proportionally weighted less than in LEED for Homes. A maximum of nine points is available in a category (Resource Efficiency) in which more than 200 points are available.

CRITERIA

After determining which items to include in the NAHB Guidelines, its developers allocated point awards based on the following priorities, in descending order of importance: first, environmental impact, and how builders can reduce the impact; second, building science and best practices, including practices that effect durability; and third, ease of implementation.[9] The categories are described in the following subsections.[10]

Lot Design, Preparation, and Development

This category focuses on selecting a site that minimizes the environmental impact of development through site selection, by minimizing site disturbance during construction, and by the way buildings are located on the site. There are 96 points available in this category, from which a minimum of 8, 10, or 12 points must be earned to achieve the bronze, silver, or gold level, respectively. There are no mandatory prerequisites in this category.

Resource Efficiency

This category includes reducing the quantity of materials needed and waste generated, increasing durability and reducing maintenance through design, and selecting renewable and other resource-efficient materials. At least 203 points are available in this category, from which a minimum of 44, 60, or 77 points must be earned to achieve the bronze, silver, or gold level, respectively. There are no mandatory prerequisites in this category.

Energy Efficiency

This category focuses on an integrated approach to energy efficiency, to include the building site, building envelope, and mechanical system. Two

Figure 5-2 Sealing ducts with mastic increases energy efficiency and improves comfort and indoor air quality. *Photo courtesy of the McKee Group.*

Figure 5-3 Raised-heel truss construction allows adequate room at the eaves for full-depth insulation to extend to the exterior wall. In this case, R-60 insulation will be installed. *Photo by Paul Norton, courtesy of DOE/NREL.*

approaches are possible for this category: the performance path and the prescriptive path. The performance path has 37, 62, or 100 points available, based on the percent (15, 30, or 40) above the 2003 International Energy Conservation Code (IECC) that the home design performs in a RES*check*™ analysis.[11] These point values correspond to the minimum requirements to reach the bronze, silver, or gold level. The alternative approach, the prescriptive path, requires the same number of points from a total of more than 300 available. For either the performance or prescriptive path, the required points at every level may be reduced by 15 if the home does not have a ducted space heating and cooling system. The reduction is owing to the lesser number of points available to homes with nonducted systems.

In addition to the minimum point requirements, homes must meet three mandatory conditions in this category:

- First, they must be equivalent to the 2003 IECC or the local energy code, whichever is more stringent.

- Second, space heating and cooling system equipment must be sized for loads using Air Conditioning Contractors of America (ACCA) Manual J or equivalent.

- Third, plan review by a third party is required to verify the design's compliance with the points sought in the Energy Efficiency section.

Figure 5-4 A low-tech system to collect and distribute rainwater.

Water Efficiency

Indoor and outdoor water conservation measures are covered in this category. There at least 92 points available—more if the project contains more than one showerhead, two faucets, and one water-using appliance—from which a minimum of 6, 13, or 19 points must be earned to achieve the bronze, silver, or gold level, respectively. There are no mandatory prerequisites in this category.

Indoor Environmental Quality

This category includes minimizing and managing potential indoor air pollutants and managing moisture. Up to 132 points are available, from which a minimum of 32, 54, and 72 points must be earned to achieve the bronze, silver, or gold level, respectively. There are no mandatory prerequisites in this category.

Operation, Maintenance, and Homeowner Education

This category focuses on providing a manual to owners or tenants detailing how to capitalize on the home's green features and describing how to properly maintain and operate their home. A maximum of 19 points are available, from which a minimum of 7 points must be earned to achieve the bronze or silver level, or 9 points to achieve the gold level. There are no mandatory prerequisites in this category.

Global Impact

The Global Impact category contains those items that, in the assessment of the NAHB Guidelines developers, did not fit neatly into one of the other categories. Its primary focus is on volatile organic compounds (VOCs) in paints and coatings. The NAHB Guidelines state that VOCs are not included in the Indoor Environmental Quality category since most of these compounds are released when the paint dries (before occupancy), yet have a negative impact on the environment.

Up to 18 points are available in this category, from which a minimum of 3, 5, or 6 points must be earned to achieve the bronze, silver, or gold level respectively. There are no mandatory prerequisites in this category.

Site Planning and Development

There are no points available in this category, although the NAHB Guidelines offer suggestions for minimizing project impact on the environment through site selection and site development at a community or subdivision scale.

Climate: Hot-Humid (Zone 3)

Size: 1,983 square feet; three bedrooms, two baths

Construction Cost: $149/square foot

Completion Date: 2008

HERS Index Score: 69

Designer: Katahdin Cedar Log Homes, Oakfield, Maine

Builder: Carolina Log Center, Lexington, South Carolina

HERS/ENERGY STAR Rater: Gilmore Consulting Services, LLC, Blythewood, South Carolina

CASE STUDY **1**

Log Home, Leesville, South Carolina

Log Home, Leesville, South Carolina 449 Points Achieved (Gold Level)	
Lot Design, Preparation, and Development	69
Resource Efficiency	104
Energy Efficiency	150
Water Efficiency	19
Indoor Environmental Quality	77
Operation, Maintenance, and Homeowner Education	19
Global Impact	11

Sustainable Features

Energy-efficient features include a conditioned crawl space (see Figure 5-5) and tankless hot water heater. A layer of rigid insulation between the interior wood panel and exterior log wall increases the thermal resistance of the wall assembly to R-14. The home also earned the ENERGY STAR for Homes label with a HERS Index score of 69.

The northern white cedar logs are insect- and mildew-resistant, and are certified by the Forest Stewardship Council. The house was located on the site to minimize the number of trees that had to be removed. The crush-and-run driveway is permeable to water.

Tips from the Builder

To construct an NAHB-program certified green home, builder Bill Seymour of the Carolina Log Center says the following are needed: "One, the desire to

Figure 5-5 The insulated crawl space improves energy efficiency. *Photo courtesy of Carolina Log Center.*

build green; two, a good rater; and three, understanding building science."[12] He adds, "I encourage all builders to at least start to take the steps to building an energy-efficient home. There are many ways we all can improve our building processes."[13]

Seymour considered LEED for Homes as well as the NAHB Guidelines, but went with the latter after concluding it was less expensive and easier to use. The costs of certification of this home included $200 to the NAHB and $125 to the local HBA. The rater's fee was $1,050.[14]

Figure 5-6 The black gasket on top of the log (right) will be compressed with the addition of the next log, creating a seal. Logs meet window and door openings with a tight seal formed by a spline and caulk. *Photo courtesy of Carolina Log Center.*

Figure 5-7 This condominium was certified silver in the Green Build Michigan program, which uses the NAHB Model Green Home Building Guidelines. *Photo courtesy of Sunrise Builders of Marquette Inc.*

CASE STUDY 2

Single-Family Condominium, Marquette, Michigan

Climate: Cold (Zone 6)

Size: 1,329 square feet; two bedrooms, two-and-a-half baths

Construction Cost: $284,691

Completion Date: 2009

HERS Index Score: 57

Designer/Builder: Sunrise Builders, Marquette, Michigan

Rater: Discovery Energy Consultants, LLC, Rapid River, Michigan

Points Achieved: 332, silver certification. The project was certified by Green Build Michigan, which uses the *NAHB Model Green Home Building Guidelines.*

Condominium, Marquette, Michigan 332 Points Achieved (Silver Level)	
Lot Design, Preparation, and Development	33
Resource Efficiency	67
Energy Efficiency	85
Water Efficiency	34
Indoor Environmental Quality	89
Operation, Maintenance, and Homeowner Education	18
Global Impact	6

Figure 5-8 The engineered hardwood floors are FSC certified. *Photo courtesy of Sunrise Builders of Marquette Inc.*

This single-family stand-alone condominium is 1 of 34, part of a much larger master-planned neighborhood. Sunrise Builders pursued certification primarily to see how its product performed compared to the ENERGY STAR and Green Build Michigan programs. "Without really changing how we would have built this home without the certifications, we found that our product performed exceptionally well. While we may not have all of our homes certified, they are all built to the same standards. The certification process and the knowledge that we have gained from this process also provides us with a powerful tool to educate our buyers as to what a high-performance, energy-efficient and 'green' home really is," said Andrea L'Huillier, Corporate Financial Manager.[15]

Additional Costs

By pursuing certification, additional expenses to Sunrise Builders—including the rater, materials, and staff time—came to about $2,000, estimates L'Huillier.[16]

Sustainable Features

Energy-efficient features include a high-efficiency furnace, tankless hot water heater, and ENERGY STAR appliances. The building envelope is tight, and features R-50 attic insulation and insulated rim joists and below-grade walls. The engineered hardwood floors are FSC-certified; lumber came from local mills. The exterior is low-maintenance, with vinyl siding and PVC trim.

Tips from the Builder

L'Huillier thinks it would be helpful for people interested in designing and building a certified home to become an NAHB Certified Green Professional. She also found the NAHB Guidelines manual to be a good resource. She adds, "The best tip that I can think of to share with other builders looking to pursue a 'green-built home' is to partner up with a rater as early on in the design process as possible. It will be tremendously easier and potentially a lot more cost-effective to learn from a good rater what the key(s) are before the design has begun."[17]

CASE STUDY 3

Custom Home,
Placitas, New Mexico

Figure 5-9 Renewable energy sources in this home include a solar thermal domestic hot water system and 3kW solar photovoltaic system. *Photo courtesy of Kayeman Custom Homes.*

Climate: Cold (Zone 4)

Size: 3,200 square feet; four bedrooms, three baths

Construction Cost: $710,000

Completion Date: 2008

HERS Index Score: 55 without solar PV system, 38 with solar PV system

Designer/Builder: Kayeman Custom Homes, Placitas, New Mexico

Rater: Building Energy Solutions, Placitas, New Mexico

Points Achieved: 530, gold

Custom Home, Placitas, New Mexico 530 Points Achieved (Gold Level)	
Lot Design, Preparation, and Development	81
Resource Efficiency	110
Energy Efficiency	175
Water Efficiency	53
Indoor Environmental Quality	73
Operation, Maintenance, and Homeowner Education	27
Global Impact	11

Figure 5-10 Located in the Albuquerque metropolitan area, this high-performance home has many traditional southwestern architectural features. *Photo courtesy of Kayeman Custom Homes.*

This home was certified under the Build Green New Mexico (BGNM) program which used the NAHB Guidelines and tailored them to account for the local climate. For example, there were more water efficiency points required than under the national guidelines. With the release of the National Green Building Standard (NGBS) in 2009, the BGNM program switched to that standard as the program's base, in part to coordinate with the state's requirements for tax credits and other incentives for sustainable building.[18]

Additional Costs

Michael Cecchini, Vice President of Kayeman, Inc, estimated the additional costs of pursuing certification, including improvements over conventional construction (exclusive of solar panels) at $7,000.[19]

Sustainable Features

Energy-efficient features include a 95 percent efficient modulated boiler for radiant heat, SEER 14 air conditioner units, a solar thermal domestic hot water system, and a 3kW solar photovoltaic (PV) system. The building envelope includes one-inch thermal house wrap (R-5.5) to mitigate thermal bridging, cellulose wall insulation (R-22), and roof deck insulation of R-22 Icynene and R-18 cellulose insulation. Water-conserving features include a grass-free xeriscape

Figure 5-11 The reflective thermal blanket under the radiant floor heating system improves energy performance. *Photo courtesy of Kayeman Custom Homes.*

with native vegetation; low-flow toilets, faucets, and showerheads; and an advanced treatment septic system.

Tips from the Builder

Cecchini emphasizes the importance of using a system that takes regional climatic differences into account, as the Build Green New Mexico program does. Although Kayeman Custom Homes are designed to meet certification requirements without the solar PV system, most clients opt to install the system. With tax credits and incentives from the utility company, a PV system designed to supply 40 to 50 percent of electricity needs results in a near-net-zero energy cost after accounting for the electric company's renewable energy credit. First costs for a solar PV system can typically be recovered in about eight years.[20]

RESOURCES

Green Building Initiative (GBI), www.thegbi.org/residential: Some regional homebuilder associations have adapted the NAHB Guidelines to the local climate, and a number of these programs are listed on the GBI website, along with links to video presentations of training for best green building practices.

NAHB National Green Building Program (NAHB Green), www.nahb-green.org: The site offers the online Green Scoring Tool, green building educational resources, a list of approved verifiers, and other information. It also lists voluntary green building programs affiliated with the NAHB Green Building Program.

NOTES

1. www.nahb.org; accessed March 26, 2009.
2. *NAHB Model Green Home Building Guidelines*, 2006, p. 1.
3. Ibid., p. 7.
4. Ibid., p. 1.
5. "Home Certification," http://nahbgreen.org/Certification/homecertification.aspx; accessed April 29, 2009.
6. "Green Home Building Rating Systems—A Sample Comparison," prepared by NAHB Research Center, Inc., March 2008, p. 11.
7. Michelle Desiderio, NAHB Research Center Director of Green Building Programs, email to the author from Anne Holtz, Director of Communications, NAHB Research Center, July 28, 2009.
8. "Verifier's Resource Guide," NAHB Research Center, 2009, p. 2.
9. *NAHB Guidelines*, p. 5.
10. Summarized from *NAHB Guidelines*, 2006.
11. RES*check* is a tool that helps designers and builders determine whether their buildings comply with the Model Energy Code, IECC, and many state energy codes. RES*check* software is available for free download from the U.S. Department of Energy website, www.energycodes.gov/rescheck.
12. Bill Seymour, Owner, Carolina Log Center, Lexington, South Carolina, email to the author, June 2, 2009.
13. Ibid.
14. Ibid., June 2, and June 8, 2009.
15. Andrea L'Huillier, Corporate Financial Manager, Sunrise Builders, email to the author, July 15, 2009.
16. Ibid.
17. Ibid.
18. Steve Hale, Director, Build Green New Mexico, email to the author, May 22, 2009.
19. Mike Cecchini, Vice President of Kayeman, Inc., email to the author, July 27, 2009.
20. Cecchini, email to the author, July 27, 2009; and telephone conversation with the author, July 30, 2009.

6

NATIONAL GREEN BUILDING STANDARD

The National Green Building Standard (NGBS)™ (ICC 700-2008) was developed by the NAHB Research Center, a subsidiary of the National Association of Home Builders (NAHB), and the International Code Council (ICC). The *NAHB Model Green Home Building Guidelines* described in the previous chapter was the starting point for the development of the NGBS, which was approved by the American National Standards Institute (ANSI) in 2009. In addition to new single-family homes, the NGBS covers multifamily homes, residential renovations and additions, and land development for subdivisions. As well as serving as a standard, it is also designed as a voluntary program which may be implemented with NAHB Research Center accredited verifiers.

The NGBS has six point categories available for green residential buildings: Lot Design, Preparation, and Development; Resource Efficiency; Energy Efficiency; Water Efficiency; Indoor Environmental Quality; and Operation, Maintenance, and Building Owner Education. Besides the threshold point requirements for each category, additional points in any category are needed to reach the four performance levels—bronze, silver, gold, and emerald—indicated in Table 6-1.

Independent of green buildings, the NGBS may be applied to new and existing subdivision sites under the Site Design and Development category.

Figure 6-1 Spray-in Icynene foam insulation acts as an air barrier as well as insulation. *Photo courtesy of Magleby Companies.*

The four levels of achievement available in this category are: one star, two stars, three stars, and four stars.

ELIGIBILITY

In contrast to the NAHB Guidelines which apply only to new single-family homes, the NGBS has a wider scope and applies to all residential projects that are not classified as institutional, and to all U.S. climate zones. Per Section 102.1, "This NGBS shall also be used for subdivisions, building

TABLE 6-1 THRESHOLD POINT RATINGS FOR GREEN BUILDINGS

Green Building Categories	Performance Level Points(1)(2)			
	Bronze	Silver	Gold	Emerald
Lot Design, Preparation, and Development	39	66	93	119
Resource Efficiency	45	79	113	146
Energy Efficiency	30	60	100	120
Water Efficiency	14	26	41	60
Indoor Environmental Quality	36	65	100	140
Operation, Maintenance, and Building Owner Education	8	10	11	12
Additional Points from any Category	50	100	100	100
Total Points	222	406	558	697

(1) In addition to the threshold number of points in each category, all mandatory provisions of each category shall be implemented.

(2) For dwelling units greater than 4,000 square feet (372 m²), the number of points in Category 7 (Additional points from any category) shall be increased in accordance with Section 601.1. The Total Points shall be increased by the same number of points.

Source: Adapted from National Green Building Standard (Washington DC: BuilderBooks, 2009) p. 12. © 2009, National Association of Home Builders. Reproduced with permission.

sites, alterations, additions, renovations, mixed-use residential buildings, and historic buildings, where applicable."

As a standard, the NGBS may be adopted by an entity as a regulation or policy. The "adopting entity" may be any third-party body that implements and administers the NGBS, such as a municipality, state, or local home-builders organization. As of mid-2009, the NGBS had been referenced as an option in several pieces of legislation, but it had not been officially adopted in any location.[1] Instead, it serves as a voluntary program, with the NAHB Research Center acting as the adopting entity for certifying homes.

THE PROCESS

If the NGBS is adopted, the adopting entity determines the certification and verification process for the standard. Otherwise, the NAHB Research Center administers the process, which is the same as that for the NAHB Guidelines (refer back to Figure 5-1). One difference is that NGBS certification may be obtained for residential land development as well as for buildings.

The NAHB Research Center describes the process as follows:[2]

1. The designer or builder enters project information using NAHB Green's online Green Scoring Tool. The tool (available for free use following registration at www.nahbgreen.org) takes users through the checklist of items that are eligible to earn points. In addition to a checkbox for claiming points for each item, there are links to additional information on how to verify the item, its intent, how to implement it, and additional resources. As the user moves through the checklist, a scorecard that tracks the anticipated points in the category is displayed, along with the total points required for each level of certification. The completed checklist, or Designer's Report, can then be exported and downloaded as an Excel spreadsheet.

2. At the start of construction, the builder selects an NAHB accredited verifier, forwards the Designer's Report to the verifier, and schedules a rough inspection with the verifier. The verifier notifies the NAHB Research Center that the rough inspection is scheduled. This marks the point at which the home enters the certification process.

3. At the conclusion of the rough inspection, the builder and verifier sign the Verification Report and the verifier sends the report to the NAHB Research Center for review. The Research Center will send the builder a Program Participation Agreement, unless an agreement with the builder is already on file from a previous project.

4. The builder pays the NAHB Research Center the green building certification fee and returns the Program Participation Agreement to the NAHB Research Center, along with proof of insurance.

5. After the verifier performs the final inspection, the final Verification Report is signed by the verifier and builder and submitted to the NAHB Research Center. The Research Center reviews the report and issues the Certified Green Home certificate to the builder.

THE COST

The cost to purchase the National Green Building Standard document is about $36. If the NGBS has been adopted by an entity, the adopting entity sets fees and verification requirements. When administered by the NAHB Research Center, there is no registration fee and the use of online tools is free, but there is a $200 certification fee per single-family home. Multifamily buildings may be certified for $200 plus $20 per unit. The cost of verification is set by individual NAHB Research Center accredited verifiers. Fees are based in part on how long the verification process is expected to take, which will vary with project size, systems complexity, and other factors. In 2008 the NAHB Research Center estimated plan review and verification costs at $750 per home for up to 10 homes, dropping to $350 per home for builders constructing more than 500 homes per year.[3]

THIRD-PARTY VERIFICATION

If the NGBS is adopted as a regulation, the adopting entity determines how compliance with the standard is to be verified. Otherwise, the NAHB Research Center acts as the adopting entity for certification. The Research Center trains, tests, and accredits all verifiers for the NGBS. A list of accredited verifiers is available at www.nahbgreen.org.

The Green Scoring Tool used to create the Designer's Report features a pop-up window for each credit that describes required documentation. It also gives instructions to the verifier regarding what to look for when verifying the credit. These instructions can be a useful resource for designers and builders, as well.

CERTIFICATION CRITERIA

The overview given in this section has been summarized from the NGBS.[4] Project teams pursuing compliance should refer to the full NGBS document as their primary resource for this information.

The criteria and mandatory requirements described in this section apply to new construction. The NGBS does cover additions and renovations, but that information is beyond the scope of this book.

Site Design and Development

This category covers land development for the future construction of, or additions to, dwelling units, including site selection, design, and construction. It applies only to the site, which is rated independently of buildings. A subdivision site may meet the NGBS requirements to be qualified as "green" whether or not the buildings on the site meet the threshold for green buildings described in the six categories that follow.

Up to a total of 292 points are available in the category for Site Design and Development. There are 79 points required to achieve the one-star performance level, 104 points for two stars, 134 points for three stars, and 175 points for four stars.

Site Design and Development Mandatory Item

In this category, the project team must create and then follow a checklist of green site development practices. This is the only mandatory requirement in this category, and it earns three points.

Lot Design, Preparation, and Development

This category applies to lot design and focuses on strategies to prevent or decrease the environmental impacts of development. Lot selection, conservation of existing natural resources, stormwater management, landscaping, and minimizing site disturbance during construction are among the items addressed.

A maximum of 233 points are available in this category, from which a minimum of 39, 66, 93, or 119 points must be earned to achieve the bronze, silver, gold, or emerald performance level, respectively. There are no mandatory requirements in this category.

Resource Efficiency

This category covers building materials and construction waste management. Points are available for reducing materials needed; for using materials that are durable, reused, renewable, indigenous, or contain recycled content; and for recycling construction waste. Up to 15 points are available for using a life-cycle assessment tool compliant with a recognized standard to select products or assemblies.

There are 274 points available for new construction, from which a minimum of 45, 79, 113, or 146 points must be earned to achieve the bronze, silver, gold, or emerald performance level, respectively.

Resource Efficiency Mandatory Items and Point Minimums

There are five mandatory items for new construction in the Resource Efficiency category.

- *Conditioned Floor Area:* One point is added to the total number required to reach each performance level for every 100 square feet of conditioned floor area greater than 4,000 square feet. Between 6 and 15 points can be earned for homes 2,500 square feet or smaller.
- *Drainage:*
  - For below-grade usable or habitable space, exterior drain tile must be installed where required by the International Building Code (IBC) and International Residential Code (IRC).
  - Finish grade must fall 6 inches within 10 feet of the building perimeter.
- *Water-Resistive Barrier:* A water-resistive barrier and/or drainage plane behind the exterior veneer or siding is mandatory where required by the IBC or IRC.
- *Ice Barrier:* In areas where ice forms along the eaves, an ice barrier is required in accordance with the IBC or IRC.

Energy Efficiency

There are two paths to achieving the required point thresholds in the Energy Efficiency category: the performance path and the prescriptive path. The one selected will depend, in part, on the level of compliance sought; projects seeking the emerald level must follow the performance path. Users must choose one path to pursue since points available in one path are not available if the other path is taken. As an alternative to the two paths, the bronze level of compliance may be reached in this category if the home is ENERGY STAR qualified.

In addition to the points available on each path, an Additional Practices group of points may be earned for either path. In each path, at least two practices must be followed. These practices include items such as energy-efficient lighting, sun-tempered design, and passive cooling design features.

Energy Efficiency Performance Path

On the performance path, 30, 60, 90, or 120 points can be earned by exceeding the energy cost performance of the ICC International Energy

Figure 6-2 The double-stud wall construction creates a thermal break for a high-performance exterior wall. This home was constructed as a net-zero energy home by Habitat for Humanity of Metro Denver, with the assistance of the National Renewable Energy Laboratory (NREL). *Photo by Paul Norton. Courtesy of DOE/NREL.*

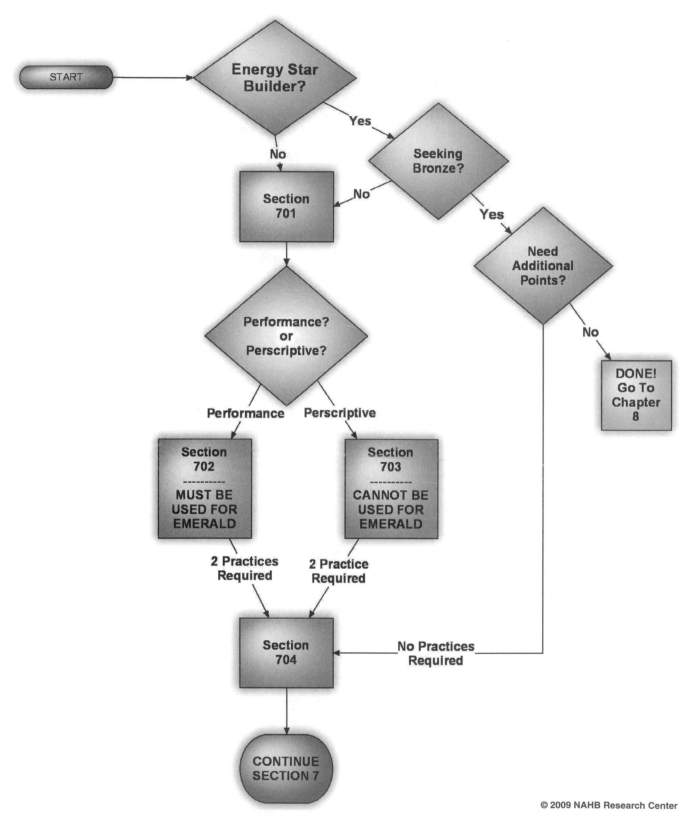

© 2009 NAHB Research Center

Figure 6-3 Diagram of pathways in the Energy Efficiency category. Section 701 addresses minimum energy-efficiency requirements. Section 702 refers to the performance path, and Section 703 to the prescriptive path. Section 704 covers additional energy-efficiency practices. *NAHB Research Center, National Green Building Certification.*

Conservation Code (IECC) baseline by 15, 30, 50, or 60 percent, respectively. The point values correspond to the minimum requirements to reach the bronze, silver, gold, or emerald performance level. Documentation demonstrating performance levels using approved software is required.

Energy Efficiency Prescriptive Path

The prescriptive requirements cover the insulation and air sealing of the building envelope, including windows, as well as the efficiency of HVAC and water heating equipment. Many requirements are climate-zone-specific. Analysis of the building envelope may be conducted through RES*check* or other software, or by third-party on-site verification. The number of points available in this path varies depending on whether or not third-party verification is employed, where the project is located, what type of heating and cooling systems are installed, and other factors.

Energy Efficiency Mandatory Items

This category has a number of mandatory requirements that must be met, beginning with these two:

- A building complying with the performance path requirements must exceed the IECC baseline performance by 15 percent.
- A building complying with the prescriptive path requirements must earn at least 30 points.

The following mandatory items apply to new construction on both the performance and prescriptive paths.

- *HVAC System:* Space heating and cooling equipment must be sized using ACCA Manual J. Radiant or hydronic space heating systems must be designed by an accredited design professional following manufacturer recommendations, or using industry-approved guidelines.
- *Duct Systems:* Ducts must be sealed in accordance with referenced standards. Building cavities may not be used as supply ducts.
- *Insulation:* Insulation must be installed properly.
- *Sealing Shafts:* Openings to unconditioned spaces must be sealed.
- *Floors:* Floors must be insulated as described.
- *Crawlspaces:* Insulation in insulated crawlspaces must be permanently attached. In unvented crawlspaces with exposed earth, measures must be taken to retard vapor transmission.
- *Walls:* Measures to provide an air barrier around doors and windows are required. Appropriate insulation and/or sealing at band and rim joists, between the sill plate and foundation, and at skylight and knee-

walls are also required. Code-required exterior wall insulation should not be interrupted by stairs, decks, and other architectural features.

■ *Ceilings and Attics:* Except in unvented attics, attic access must be insulated. Recessed lighting penetrating the thermal envelope must meet stated requirements. Where eave vents exist, measures to minimize air movement through or under the insulation must be employed.

■ *Fenestration:* Exterior doors, windows, and all skylights must meet ENERGY STAR or equivalent specifications for the climate region.

Water Efficiency

This category focuses on strategies to reduce water usage, both indoors and outdoors. Measures include the installation of water-conserving appliances, fixtures, faucets, and irrigation systems, and rainwater collection and use.

There are up to about 155 points available for new construction in this category, from which a minimum of 14, 26, 41, or 60 points must be earned to achieve the bronze, silver, gold, or emerald performance level, respectively.

Water Efficiency Mandatory Items and Point Minimums

The water efficiency category has one mandatory item. That is, to reach the gold or emerald performance levels, all water closets and urinals must either meet stated maximum flush volumes or be composting or waterless fixtures.

Indoor Environmental Quality

This category focuses on controlling pollutants and pollutant sources, and on managing moisture. Items include the location of different space and water heating equipment; the emissivity of interior finish materials and sealants; ventilation systems; and moisture control measures that inhibit the growth of mold, among other benefits.

There are roughly 200 points available for new construction in this category, a number that varies depending on specific building features, systems, and location. From this total, a minimum of 36, 65, 100, or 140 points must be earned to achieve the bronze, silver, gold, or emerald performance level, respectively.

Indoor Environmental Quality Mandatory Items

There are 13 mandatory items for new construction in this category, although not all will apply to every project.

■ *Fireplaces and Fuel-Burning Appliances:* Fireplaces and fuel-burning appliances, such as fireplaces, fireplace inserts, pellet (biomass) stoves and furnaces, wood stoves, and masonry heaters, located in conditioned spaces must have adequate combustion and ventilation air, be code-compliant and vent to the outdoors. Either 6 or 7 points are available for meeting this requirement, depending on the type of fireplace or fuel-burning appliance.

- *Attached Garages*—The door between the garage and the conditioned space must be sealed and gasketed (2 points). Also, there must be a continuous air barrier between the walls and ceiling separating the garage and conditioned living spaces (2 points).

- *Wood Materials*—Structural plywood and OSB used for floor, wall, or roof sheathing must meet cited performance standards.

- *Carpets:* Wall-to-wall carpeting may not be installed next to water closets or bathing fixtures.

- *Spot Ventilation—Bathrooms:* Bathrooms must be vented to the outdoors and meet minimum ventilation rates.

- *Spot Ventilation—Clothes Dryers:* Clothes dryers must be vented to the outdoors.

- *Radon Control:* Buildings in the U.S. Environmental Protection Agency (EPA) Radon Zones 1 and 2 must have a radon system (10 or 15 points).

- *Tile Backing Materials:* In wet areas, the backing materials installed under tile must comply with referenced standards.

- *Capillary Breaks:* A capillary break and vapor retarder must be installed at all concrete slabs in accordance with one of three options listed in the NGBS.

- *Crawlspaces:* Crawlspace walls below the finish grade must be damp-proofed.

- *Moisture Control Measures:* Insulation with a high moisture content must be allowed to dry before the wall is enclosed.

- *Duct Insulation:* In all unconditioned spaces, all HVAC ducts, trunks, and plenums must be insulated to a minimum of R6.

Operation, Maintenance, and Homeowner Education

This category seeks to ensure that the building owners and operators are informed about the building's maintenance, operation, and green components. Measures include providing a manual that lists the building's green attributes; presents a green building program certificate; and offers information on installed appliances, equipment, and fixtures. The requirements for one- and two-family dwellings are different from those for multifamily dwellings. From the total available for each building type, a minimum of 8, 10, 11, or 12 points must be earned to achieve the bronze, silver, gold, or emerald performance level, respectively. For one- and two-family dwellings, up to 10 points are available for providing an owner's manual.

There are three mandatory items in this category, and additional points may be earned for including information on 17 other items, such as public transportation options, humidity control, and gutter and downspout maintenance.

For multifamily buildings, some 13 points may be earned for providing a building construction manual, operations manual, and maintenance manual. Copies of the manuals must be distributed to all "responsible parties," including the owner, tenant, maintenance team, and management.[5]

Operation, Maintenance, and Homeowner Education Mandatory Items

In the Operation, Maintenance, and Homeowner Education category, there are three mandatory items applicable to the building owners' manual for one- and two-family homes, each of which earns one-half point:

- A green building program certificate or completion document
- A list of green building features
- Product data and manufacturer's manuals for equipment, fixtures, and appliances.

There are seven mandatory items for multiunit homes, each of which earns one-half point:

- *Building Construction Manual:* The three mandatory items in this manual are: (1) a list of green attributes in the building, with a narrative describing the importance of green construction; (2) a copy of the NGBS as adopted by the local jurisdiction, the measures achieved by the particular building, and a certificate from the local green building program; and (3) maintenance, operation, and warranty information on installed fixtures, appliances, equipment, and fixtures.

- *Operations Manual:* This manual also has three mandatory items: (1) a narrative about living in and using a green home; (2) a list of ways to save energy and water; and (3) strategies for maintaining humidity at prescribed levels.

- *Maintenance Manual:* The Maintenance Manual must describe the importance of properly maintaining a green building.

Climate: Mixed-Humid (Zone 3)

Size: 1,873 square feet; three bedrooms, two baths

Estimated Sales Price: $225,000

Completion Date: 2009

Designer: Design Studio Inc., Ridgeland, Mississippi

Builder: David Smith Builder, Inc., Ridgeland, Mississippi

Verifier: Gary N. Smith, Ridgeland, Mississippi

Points Achieved: 260, bronze certification

CASE STUDY 1

Custom Home,
Madison, Mississippi

Custom Home, Madison, Mississippi 260 Points Achieved (Bronze Level)	
Lot Design, Preparation, and Development	45
Resource Efficiency	78
Energy Efficiency	35
Water Efficiency	18
Indoor Environmental Quality	73
Operation, Maintenance, and Homeowner Education	11

David Smith built this house for the Home Builders Association of Jackson's annual fund-raiser for the Batson Hospital for Children in Jackson, Mississippi. Smith estimates the additional costs for constructing a green home were $2,500 more than for a conventional home, including the $200 fee to the NAHB. The verifier and designer donated their services; the lot was also donated.

Smith had already built several homes that were certified under the NAHB Model Green Home Building Guidelines and found the NAHB Guidelines easier to meet. "Standard points are harder to earn," he said, adding, "The standard has more teeth in it. It's way better in the places it should be," offering higher point rewards for more expensive items like more efficient HVAC equipment and improved energy—items that ultimately offer a larger return for consumers.[6]

Sustainable Features

Among the sustainable features that earned points were an open lot that didn't require tree removal and allowed for good site orientation; proper wrapping, flashing, and proper sealing of pipes and wires—"basic means of construction that we normally use, but a little better," said Smith; efficient equipment properly located, with sealed ductwork, compact fluorescent lighting, and ENERGY STAR fans and appliances; a tankless hot water heater in proximity to the maniblock system for efficient water distribution; and low-VOC caulks and adhesives. A third-party verifier performed a blower door test and duct-blaster test. Smith opted not to pay an additional $700 for low-VOC paint, saying that while he understood the environmental and health benefits, it was unlikely to add enough value to the home to justify the additional expense.[7]

Tips from the Builder

Smith encourages builders aspiring to build green homes to get as much education in green building as they can. He described the NAHB Certified Green Builder™ program as a good entry-level program, but said that more knowledge is required to build a green home. He also said builders should be prepared to spend time administering the certification requirements. "It's very time-consuming to get online and score the house," he said.[8]

CASE STUDY 2

Production Home,
Valparaiso, Indiana

Figure 6-4 Among the strategies used for achieving silver certification was locating the home on the lot so as to minimize the environmental impact of development. *Photo courtesy of Coolman Communities, Inc.*

Figure 6-5 Coolman Communities expects this home to perform 50 percent better than the local standard for energy efficiency. *Photo courtesy of Coolman Communities, Inc.*

Climate: Cold (Zone 5)

Size: Finished: 1,920 square feet: three bedrooms, two-and-a half baths; unfinished: 960-square-foot basement and 330-square-foot bonus room over the two-car garage.

Sales Price: $254,744

Completion Date: 2009

HERS Index Score: 66

Designer/Builder: Coolman Communities, Inc., Valparaiso, Indiana

Verifier: Energy Diagnostics, Valparaiso, Indiana

Mechanical Contractor: G.L. Jorgensen HVAC, Valparaiso, Indiana

Insulation Contractor: Energy-Tech Insulation, Valparaiso, Indiana

Points Achieved: 498 points, silver certification

Production Home, Valparaiso, Indiana 498 Points Achieved (Silver Level)	
Lot Design, Preparation, and Development	115
Resource Efficiency	114
Energy Efficiency	103
Water Efficiency	42
Indoor Environmental Quality	112
Operation, Maintenance, and Homeowner Education	12

This home is built in a green subdivision, certified under the NGBS at the three-star level for site design and development.

Sustainable Features

Sustainable strategies were implemented by carefully planning how to locate the home on the lot, finding materials that earned NGBS points without adding greatly to the cost, and providing slightly higher efficiency HVAC equipment.

Tips from the Builder

Kelly Kaminski, Production Manager of Coolman Communities, says that becoming a Certified Green Professional through the NAHB lends credibility. She further suggests:[9]

- ■ "Those wanting to design or build a certified home should first gain an over-all knowledge of sound, efficient building principles (not generally accepted principles), and a thorough understanding that it is an 'overall system' rating and not a 'feature-rich' rating (solar panels, composting toilets, etc.), which can be achieved by a lot of research that enables you to provide product that does not drive the cost upwards.

- ■ "Educate, educate, educate! Through your builders association or local media, educate your local market to the fact that green isn't just 'curly light-bulbs and recycling.' Educate local appraisers and realtors to the program. Explain why this home will retain or gain in appraised value. Market the fact that utility costs *should* be lower, not *will* be lower. Market on the 'feel good' value, as well as the intrinsic value.

- ■ "Do your homework. It isn't easy, and it takes time. Have at least one person on staff that you can point to as your expert and make sure they continue to educate themselves as this market evolves. That education has to be extended to subs and suppliers. It is crucial that everyone is on the same page, knowing exactly what part they play in the rating process, and how they can potentially affect the entire process."

Figure 6-6 This home's tight building envelope, which features low-e windows and Icynene insulation, helped it earn silver certification and the ENERGY STAR. *Photo courtesy of Magleby Companies.*

Climate: Cold (Zone 5)

Size: 5,361 square feet finished space, plus a 3,262-square-foot basement and three-car garage; five bedrooms, four-and-a-half baths

Construction Cost: $850,000

Completion Date: 2009

HERS Score: 57

Architect: Pontis Architectural Group, Lindon, Utah

Builder: Magleby Companies, Lindon, Utah

Green and Energy Inspector: Wasatch Energy Engineering, Park City, Utah

Points Achieved: 511 points, silver certification

Custom Home, Highland, Utah 511 Points Achieved (Silver Level)	
Lot Design, Preparation, and Development	121
Resource Efficiency	95
Energy Efficiency	122
Water Efficiency	30
Indoor Environmental Quality	130
Operation, Maintenance, and Homeowner Education	13

Project Manager Jeff Atkinson of Magleby Companies says his team sought certification on this project because, "We want to provide a better product for our client."[10] He says many of the features in the certified home are standard practice for the company.

Sustainable Features

Sustainable features include a heat recovery system, power-direct vent water heater, high-efficiency HVAC equipment, ENERGY STAR appliances, compact fluorescent lightbulbs, and a tight building envelope that has low-e coated windows and Icynene insulation. The home also earned the ENERGY STAR.

Tips from the Builder

Atkinson has two suggestions for making the scoring process more efficient:[11]

- "When I first got on the online scoring tool, its length was intimidating. It took a long time to complete it," Atkinson says. He later developed a system for several different levels of certification and he uses these existing templates as a base for new projects. He copies and modifies scorecards and tailors them to new projects, resulting in great time savings over beginning with a blank scorecard.

▲ **Figure 6-7** To enhance durability and reduce maintenance, the NGBS rewards roof water discharge systems that carry water a minimum of five feet from foundation walls. *Photo courtesy of Magleby Companies.*

▶ **Figure 6-8** The high-efficiency HVAC equipment in this home includes a heat recovery ventilator and natural gas furnace. *Photo courtesy of Magleby Companies.*

■ While Atkinson finds the NGBS book useful, he thinks the scoring tool contains more information about the intent, how to implement the credit, and resources. Atkinson created a PDF file containing this information for each credit, thereby providing a readily accessible resource for himself, his site superintendent, and other users.

RESOURCES

NAHB National Green Building Program (NAHB Green), www.nahbgreen.org: This program was launched in 2008 by the NAHB Research Center. It offers the online Green Scoring Tool, green building educational resources, and a green home certification program.

National Green Building Standard: This document includes information on the scope of the standard and lists all the credits and mandatory requirements. It is available for purchase from several online booksellers.

RES*check*, www.energycodes.gov/rescheck: Training tool and free software.

U.S. Department of Energy (DOE), www.buildingamerica.gov/challenge: This website describes a Builders Challenge, launched in 2008, calling for the homebuilding industry to construct 220,000 high-performance homes by 2012. Homes in the program must be at least 30 percent more efficient than new homes built to minimum code requirements. The DOE's goal is to support the homebuilding industry in achieving cost-neutral, net-zero energy homes (those that generate as much energy as they use over the course of a year) by 2030. The DOE provides marketing tools, green building research, and other resources. When specific criteria are met, houses certified under the National Green Building Standard can qualify concurrently with the Builders Challenge.

NOTES

1. Michelle Desiderio, NAHB Research Center Director of Green Building Programs, email to the author sent by Anne Holtz, Director of Communications, NAHB Research Center, July 28, 2009.
2. "Home Certification," http://nahbgreen.org/Certification/homecertification.aspx; accessed April 29, 2009.
3. "Green Home Building Rating Systems—A Sample Comparison," prepared by NAHB Research Center, Inc., March 2008, p. 11.
4. National Green Building Standard™ (ICC 700-2008), National Association of Home Builders, 2009.

5. Ibid., p. 85.
6. David Smith, telephone interview with the author, July 27, 2009.
7. Ibid.
8. Ibid.
9. Kelly Kaminski, Production Manager, Coolman Communities, email to the author, July 31, 2009.
10. Jeff Atkinson, Project Manager, Magleby Companies, telephone conversation with the author, July 27, 2009.
11. Ibid.

7

LOCAL AND REGIONAL RESIDENTIAL PROGRAMS

The city of Austin, Texas, was a lonesome trailblazer when it established its green building program in 1991, but since the late 1990s the number of local and state government programs has mushroomed. Some provide voluntary guidelines or incentives while others mandate energy-saving or other sustainable features through legislation or regulations. In 2007, the American Institute of Architects (AIA) studied 606 of the 661 U.S. cities with populations of 50,000 or greater and found that 14 percent had some type of green building program.[1] A 2008 AIA survey of the 200 most populous counties in the United States found that nearly 20 percent (representing more than half of the nation's population) reported having a green building program for municipal, commercial, or residential construction.[2]

EXAMPLES OF LOCAL AND REGIONAL RESIDENTIAL PROGRAMS

Many localities with green residential building programs offer voluntary guidelines and incentives, such as expedited permitting, lower permit fees, or awards programs. Others require that construction comply with existing building assessment systems or with criteria unique to the locale. Here are examples of some local and regional programs.

Baltimore County, Maryland

Baltimore County, Maryland, requires that all single-family and multifamily new construction and gut-rehab projects earn the ENERGY STAR® label. The county recommends that all new affordable housing (single-family and multifamily) also achieve a minimum of LEED® Silver certification. Multifamily projects of 10,000 square feet or greater must achieve LEED Silver or higher.

Frisco, Texas

Frisco, Texas, lays claim to being the first U.S. city to mandate a residential green building program, which it instituted in 2001 and revised in 2007. The program focuses on energy and water conservation, waste and pollution reduction, and sustainable development. In addition to meeting other city codes and ordinances, new single-family residences must earn the ENERGY STAR label or a HERS Index score of 83 or lower, meet prescriptive requirements for outdoor irrigation, comply with ventilation and indoor air quality requirements, and reduce construction waste.

Health House Builder Program

Health House® is a program of the American Lung Association of the Upper Midwest®. Its focus is on indoor air quality and energy efficiency. Measures include moisture control, humidity control, whole-house ventilation, high-efficiency air filtration, and a tight building envelope. The Lung Association estimates that complying with Health House guidelines will increase construction costs by 3 to 5 percent but lower utility bills from 30 to 40 percent. Builders must work with a rater to commission the home and verify that guidelines were followed.

Irvine, California

The city of Irvine, California, has developed a voluntary program with a 100-point rating systems with which single-family homes and apartments may be "green certified." There are eight mandatory items for homes and six for apartments. A minimum score of 50 is required for certification, with three levels of achievement available. Point categories are Site and Landscape; Foundation, Frame, and Roofing; Plumbing; Lighting and Appliances; HVAC; Energy Performance; Renewable Energy; Indoor Air Quality; Resource-Efficient Materials; and Education and Awareness.

Northern California

GreenPoint Rated is a voluntary third-party-verified rating system used in many parts of Northern California. Guidelines and checklists are available for new and existing single-family and multifamily homes. It is intended to be complementary to other rating programs, like LEED for Homes and ENERGY STAR, but tailored to Northern California in areas such as water efficiency and landscaping. Rated categories are Community and Design; Site/Landscaping; Water Efficiency; Energy Efficiency; Renewable Energy; Resource Conservation; Indoor Air Quality; Durability/Moisture Control; and Innovation. The program is offered by Build It Green, a nonprofit membership organization.

Florida

The Florida Green Building Coalition (FGBC) is a nonprofit membership organization that offers five voluntary building certification programs, including the Florida Green Home Designation Standard for new and existing construction. Required qualifications include attaining at least 100 of 300 possible points, meeting or exceeding the minimum standards of the Florida energy code, and receiving third-party certification from an FGBC accredited agent. Program categories are Energy; Water; Lot Choice; Site; Health; Materials; Disaster Mitigation; and General (which includes a small house credit and renewable power generation credit).

Minnesota

Minnesota GreenStar Green Homes and Remodeling is a voluntary third-party-verified rating system offered by the nonprofit MN GreenStar. Point categories are Energy Efficiency; Resource Efficiency (Including Durability); Indoor Environmental Quality; Water Conservation; and Site and Community. Three levels of certification are available. The program is aligned with ENERGY STAR for Homes. All GreenStar-certified homes are eligible to receive the ENERGY STAR label.

Green Building Programs in Our Nation's Communities

In 2007, the AIA contacted 661 cities with populations of 50,000 or more and spoke to representatives of 606 of these cities. They compiled their findings in a report titled, "Local Leaders in Sustainability: A Study of Green Building Programs in Our Nation's Communities." Information collected on residential programs in these communities is listed in Table 7-1, for which the AIA provided updated information in 2009.

TABLE 7-1 LOCAL AND REGIONAL GREEN BUILDING PROGRAMS FOR RESIDENTIAL CONSTRUCTION

City, State	Year Program Began	Applies to: 1—Multifamily 2—Single-Family	Website	Notes
Scottsdale, Arizona	1998	1, 2	www.scottsdaleaz.gov/greenbuilding	The city requires LEED Gold for municipal buildings, and periodically updates its checklists to stay current with technology.
Anaheim, California	2007	1, 2	www.anaheim.net (Department of Public Utilities/Green Connection)	
Berkeley, California	2004	1, 2	www.cityofberkeley.info/sustainable	The city is also looking into pushing their energy requirements beyond Title 24.
Burbank, California	2003	1, 2	www.burbankca.org/building/bgreen.htm	It started as a voluntary program. The ratings are 3-tiered and focus more on getting developers to participate rather than worry about the level that is actually attained.
Cathedral City, California	2008	2	www.cathedralcity.gov	Voluntary program based on the Green Builder Program established by the California Builders Industry Institute. Incentives include expedited review and inspections and recognition of the builder as a Green Builder.
Chula Vista, California		2		
Corona, California	2007	1, 2		Based on California Green Builder Program. Incentives provided by expedited permitting.
Costa Mesa. California	2007	1, 2	www.ci.costa-mesa.ca.us/departments/greenbuilding/green-bldg.htm	Program is voluntary. LEED is referenced.
Davis, California		1, 2	www.cityofdavis.org/cdd/green_building.cfm	Build It Green is the standard for residential projects. Davis is a no-growth community.
Irvine, California	2006	1, 2		Irvine has its own 100 pt. rating system for commercial and residential recognition.
Livermore, California	2006	1, 2	In development	The mandatory program will require 20 LEED points for commercial and 50 Build It Green Points for residential.
Mission Viejo, California	2006	1, 2	http://cityofmissionviejo.org/depts/cd/green_building	The program is still in its pilot phase until 2008.
Novato, California	2005	2	www.ci.novato.ca.us/cd/forms/CDP047.htm	The policy is mandatory for new construction and requires 50 Green Points.
Pasadena, California	2006	1	www.ci.pasadena.ca.us/permitcenter/greencity/building/gbprogram.asp	Public buildings, 25,0001 sq. ft. commercial, and 41 story residential projects are required to be LEED certified. It is optional for other development.

(continued)

TABLE 7-1 (*Continued*)

City, State	Year Program Began	Applies to: 1–Multifamily 2–Single-Family	Website	Notes
Petaluma, California	2006	1, 2	www.cityofpetaluma.net/cdd/big/index.html	The program is optional for all and there is a $500 per unit rebate incentive.
Pleasanton, California	2002	1, 2	www.ci.pleasanton.ca.us/business/planning	The mandatory portions of the program were passed in 2006, before this it only applied to municipal buildings.
Redding, California	2005	2	www.reupower.com/energysvc/earth-adv.asp	The Earth Advantage program used Portland as its model. The city owns the electric company so many initiatives concern energy.
Riverside, California	2007	2		The program is brand new as of summer.
San Diego, California	2002	1	www.sandiego.gov/environmental-services/sustainable/index.shtml	San Diego's program comprises a number of ordinances requiring municipal buildings be LEED Silver and providing expedited planning incentives to commercial and multifamily developments.
San Francisco, California	1999	1	www.sfenvironment.org/our_programs/overview.html?ssi=8	The city is continuing to advance. This summer the Green Task Force recommended a number of changes, including mandatory standards.
San Leandro, California	2006			San Leandro builders also receive incentives from Alameda county.
San Rafael, California	2007	1, 2	In development	New mandatory program.
Santa Barbara, California	2006	1, 2	www.builtgreensb.org	The policies are voluntary for private development, and permits can be fast-tracked. There is also a solar recognition program to promote the use of solar energy.
Santa Cruz, California	2006	1, 2	www.ci.santa-cruz.ca.us/pl/building/green.html	Mandatory minimums combined with incentives.
Santa Rosa, California	2004	2		The city is considering updates to the program to strengthen it and expand its scope.
Walnut Creek, California		1, 2		Voluntary program using LEED and Build It Green. Looking to make mandatory in 2010, to follow the state level voluntary regulations of the International Green Building Council.
Boulder, Colorado	1993	2		The residential Green Points system they use is currently being updated again and will likely include commercial and multifamily housing.

(continued)

TABLE 7-1 (*Continued*)

City, State	Year Program Began	Applies to: 1–Multifamily 2–Single-Family	Website	Notes
Lauderhill, Florida	2006	1, 2		Compliance is voluntary, but all applicable buildings must submit a statement identifying any green design components.
North Miami, Florida		1, 2	www.greennorthmiami.com	Voluntary program. Incentives for LEED and other green building programs for residential projects.
St. Petersburg, Florida	2006	1, 2	www.stpete.org/development/ developmentreview.htm	Sarasota County is very active in promoting green building. The city program is very informal, but there is a very good relationship between developers, planners, and normal citizens.
West Palm Beach, Florida		1, 2		Voluntary standards that incorporate some LEED requirements.
Aurora, Illinois		1, 2		Voluntary program using LEED. Incentives include review timeframes and density and lot coverage.
Chicago, Illinois	2004	1, 2	www.cityofchicago.org (City Departments, Department of Environment)	The success of separate programs is unique to the political culture of the city and the mayor.
Bloomington, Indiana	2007	1, 2	www.bloomington.in.gov/planning	The city offers bonus density to qualified projects and also has a Green Acres neighborhood program.
Baltimore, Maryland	2008	1, 2	www.baltimorecity.gov/sustainability	All new construction over a certain size must be LEED certified "or comparable."
Rockville, Maryland	2010	1, 2	www.rockvillemd.gov/environment/ built/codes.html	All building over 7,000 sq ft must meet LEED-certified levels but need not be certified.
Boston, Massachusetts	2007	1	www.bostongreenbuilding.org	The program is written into the municipal code as Article 80. The city amended the LEED guidelines to include city-specific points for features the community values.
Bloomington, Minnesota	2005	1	www.ci.bloomington.mn.us/code/ Code19_9.html#b19_29 see Section 19.29 (g) (4) (F)	Section G-4-F in the code offers a floor area bonus for a specific zoning district. The city tried to promote mixed-use development for more walkability.
St. Paul, Minnesota	2005	1, 2		The city uses ENERGY STAR guidelines for residential. Large commercial structures must go through the Excel Energy program.

(continued)

TABLE 7-1 (*Continued*)

City, State	Year Program Began	Applies to: 1—Multifamily 2—Single-Family	Website	Notes
Springfield, Missouri		2	www.springfieldmo.gov/egov/ planning_development/index.html	Promotion of ENERGY STAR for housing projects. Low-income housing projects receiving community block grants are using some aspects of the ENERGY STAR program. Incentives through tax abatements; longer time period available for green buildings; city pays for inspections.
Las Vegas, Nevada	2006	2	www.sustainlasvegas.com (Not until the end of August)	Las Vegas has established a green building fund to raise money from utility fees and provide grants to cover LEED costs.
Elizabeth, New Jersey		1, 2		The city has a great Urban Enterprise Zone, complete with mass transit. There is also an excellent grant program for low-income housing. Over the past 15 years or so the downtown area has been completely revitalized.
Wilmington, North Carolina	2005	1, 2	www.stewardshipdev.com	Currently, the Lower Cape Fear Stewardship Development Award Program is voluntary and only provides a building award as an incentive.
Winston-Salem, North Carolina	2006	1	www.cityofws.org/Home/ Departments/Planning/Legacy/ Articles/LegacyToolkit	Winston-Salem is a Sierra Club Cool City. They are currently focused on mixed-use planning and walkability.
Cincinnati, Ohio	2006	1, 2	www.cincinnati-oh.gov/cdap/ pages/-16936	Cincinnati provides a property tax abatement for private developers. The city is also working with a developer to construct a 68-acre neighborhood to help gather data on pervious pavement and green roofs, in particular.
Cuyahoga Falls, Ohio	2005	1, 2		The city provides a density bonus for green development.
Hamilton, Ohio	2007	1		For LEED projects the city amended the code to allow a density bonus and reduced landscaping requirements.
Portland, Oregon	2000	1, 2	www.portlandonline.com/osd	One of the few cities in the country to require new municipal buildings to be Gold-rated.
Nashville-Davidson (balance), Tennessee	2007	1		Municipal buildings over 2000 sq. ft. and $2 million must be LEED Certified. Other projects are offered density bonuses to meet the same standard.
Austin, Texas	1991	1, 2	www.ci.austin.tx.us/citymgr/default.htm	The program has been around so long it is just an accepted part of the building process. Planning and permitting have a lot of flexibility with what to offer developers depending on the part of the city they will be in.

(*continued*)

TABLE 7-1 (*Continued*)

City, State	Year Program Began	Applies to: 1–Multifamily 2–Single-Family	Website	Notes
Flower Mound, Texas	2004	1, 2	www.flower-mound.com/ env_resources/envresources_ greenbuilding.php	The program is purely voluntary and offers recognition to applicable buildings.
Frisco, Texas	2001	1, 2	www.friscotexas.gov/ Projects_ProgramsGreen_Building/ ?id=155	Residential construction must meet ENERGY STAR standards. Municipal construction must be LEED Silver and Commercial or multifamily buildings have a Frisco-specific standard based on LEED.
Houston, Texas	2004	2	www.houstonpowertopeople.com	The city places an emphasis on cooperation between developers and planners. The Quick Start program is designed to provide consultation and the Houston Hope program targets low-income housing.
San Antonio, Texas	2004	2	www.buildsagreen.org/BuildSAGreen	The city works with Build San Antonio Green, a program similar to the residential policies in Madison and Atlanta, to recognize and market green housing.
Arlington CDP, Virginia	2000	1	www.arlingtonva.us/Departments/ EnvironmentalServices/epo/ EnvironmentalServicesEpoGreen Buildings.aspx#ACinc	All site plan projects must submit a LEED Scorecard and employ a LEED-accredited professional. Certain projects are required to earn 26 points; failure to do so results in a $.03 per sq. ft. fee that is used for green building education.
Seattle, Washington	2000	1, 2	www.seattle.gov/environment	In addition to the requirements for city development, Seattle has a dizzying array of incentives for all kinds of sustainable features.
Madison, Wisconsin	1999	2	www.cityofmadison.com/ Environment/default.htm	The driving principle behind the sustainable development is to earn payback on the investments within 10 years. There is more focus on partnerships as opposed to policies. They view education as the best incentive.

Source: Excerpted from Brooks Rainwater and Martin Cooper, *Local Leaders in Sustainability: A Study of Green Building Programs in Our Nation's Communities* (Washington, DC: American Institute of Architects, 2007). Reprinted by permission.

EXAMPLES OF NATIONWIDE RESIDENTIAL PROGRAMS

In addition to the widely recognized residential green building programs such as LEED for Homes, ENERGY STAR, and the National Green Building Standard™ discussed elsewhere in this book, there is a growing number of green building programs to meet the demand for green building guidelines and certification for residential construction. Some are offered by for-profit entities; others are sponsored by not-for-profit or government organizations. A selection of the latter are summarized here.

Enterprise Green Communities

Enterprise Green Communities is a national program for affordable housing launched in 2004 by Enterprise Community Partners, Inc. To be eligible for program grants, loans, and tax-credit equity, projects must meet up to 38 mandatory criteria (several may be waived based on project-specific conditions) and at least 30 of the 136 available optional criteria. Categories include Integrated Design; Site, Location and Neighborhood Fabric; Site Improvements; Water Conservation; Energy Efficiency; Materials Beneficial to the Environment; Healthy Living Environment; Operations and Maintenance. Affordable housing has been built under this program in more than 20 states, from California to Maine. The 2008 revision is intended to align the program with LEED for Homes. Intervale Green, a case study in Chapter 3, and Pearl Place, a case study in Chapter 4, participated in this program.

Building America Builders Challenge

The U.S. Department of Energy (DOE)'s Builders Challenge, launched in 2008, calls for the homebuilding industry to construct 220,000 high-performance homes by 2012. Homes in the program must be at least 30 percent more efficient than new homes built to minimum code requirements. Third-party verification is required. The DOE's goal is to support the home-building industry in achieving cost-neutral, net-zero energy homes (homes that generate as much energy as they use over the course of a year) by 2030. The DOE provides marketing tools, green building research, and other resources. When specific criteria are met, houses certified under the National Green Building Standard (see Chapter 6) can qualify concurrently with the Builders Challenge.

Living Building Challenge

The Living Building Challenge is a program of the Cascadia Region Green Building Council, a chapter of the nonprofit U.S. Green Building Council, intended for use in any location and building type. It uses as a benchmark what is possible, with the goal of creating self-sustaining buildings that generate their own renewable energy and capture and treat water. There are six performance areas, or "petals": Site, Energy, Materials, Water, Indoor Quality, and Beauty + Inspiration. There are 16 prerequisites within the performance areas; nothing is optional. A petal may be earned by complying with the requirements of that performance area. By meeting requirements for all six areas, the building can earn Living Building status; buildings must be operating for a year before being evaluated, as the designation is based on actual performance.

Passive House/Passivhaus Institut

The Passivehaus Institut was founded in Darmstadt, Germany, in 1996 as an independent research institute to develop highly efficient energy use. It developed Passivhaus (or Passive House), a construction standard for residential and nonresidential buildings without a conventional heating system that are comfortable to inhabit year-round. The standard requires a very tight building envelope and sets low annual energy use limits on a kilowatts per square foot basis. It offers a design tool, the Passive House Planning Package (PHPP), to assist in energy and other calculations necessary to achieve this end. The tool is available in several languages. The Passive House Institute U.S. provides training and certifies buildings in the United States.

RESOURCES

Local planning or building departments are good resources for information on local or state green building programs, as are departments of the environment or sustainability. Other resources are listed here.

American Institute of Architects (AIA), www.aia.org: The AIA has issued a series of reports with the main title "Local Leaders in Sustainability," covering topics such as green building programs, green counties, green incentives, and green schools.

Database of State Incentives for Renewables & Efficiency, www.dsireusa.org: Lists state, local, utility, and federal incentives for renewable energy and energy efficient measures.

Green Building Links page of the U.S. Green Building Council website, www.usgbc.org: Includes links to different government initiatives (at all levels of government) related to green buildings.

National Association of Counties (NACO), www.naco.org: NACO maintains a searchable online database of county green programs, policies, and other data.

National Association of Home Builders (NAHB), www.nahbgreen.org: NAHB maintains an online list of state and local programs affiliated with the NAHB Green Building Program. The website also provides links to green building resources for policymakers and legislators.

U.S. Department of Energy (DOE), http://eere.buildinggreen.com: The DOE sponsors a High Performance Building Database that can be searched by building type and size, location, owner name, or project name. Building information categories are: Overview; Process; Finance; Land Use; Site & Water; Energy; Materials; Indoor Environment; Images; Ratings & Awards; Lessons; and Learn More. New projects may also be submitted for inclusion.

U.S. Environmental Protection Agency Clean Energy Clean Energy-Environment State and Local Programs, www.epa.gov/cleanenergy/energy-programs: Here you'll find tools and technical assistance to state and local governments in their clean energy efforts.

NOTES

1. Brooks Rainwater, with Cooper Martin, "Local Leaders in Sustainability: A Study of Green Building Programs in Our Nation's Communities" (Washington, DC: American Institute of Architects, 2007), p. 4.

2. Brooks Rainwater and Cooper Martin, "Local Leaders in Sustainability: Green Counties" (Washington, DC: American Institute of Architects, 2008), p. 4.

8

ENERGY STAR FOR COMMERCIAL BUILDINGS

ENERGY STAR® for Buildings and Plants is a voluntary program of the U.S. Environmental Protection Agency (EPA) and Department of Energy (DOE), launched in 1995. It rates buildings for energy use intensity. To qualify for the ENERGY STAR, buildings are benchmarked against a database of similar buildings for the purpose of rating designed or actual energy consumption against actual energy use in a peer group of buildings. This performance-based comparison is in contrast to ASHRAE Standard 90.1, which compares against a baseline model. ENERGY STAR considers the energy performance of the whole building, rather than an independent assessment of the efficiency of lights, equipment, and other components. The EPA and DOE charge no fees for participation in the commercial buildings program.

Projects receiving a score of 75 or better out of a possible 100 points (indicating they are in the top 25 percent for energy performance) are eligible to earn the ENERGY STAR. Some ENERGY STAR tools can be used to track water use, but the award is based solely on energy use. There are no certification levels; that is, a building achieving a rating of 99 will earn the same ENERGY STAR label as a building with a rating of 75.

Two ENERGY STAR labels are available for commercial projects: ENERGY STAR and Designed to Earn the ENERGY STAR. The ENERGY STAR is awarded to new or existing buildings after one year of utility bills have

Figure 8-1 The ENERGY STAR label is recognized by 76 percent of American households. *Image courtesy of U.S. Environmental Protection Agency.*

123

DESIGNED TO EARN THE ENERGY STAR

The estimated energy performance for this design meets US EPA criteria. The building will be eligible for ENERGY STAR after maintaining superior performance for one year.

Figure 8-2 The EPA will email this image to the project's architect of record for inclusion on the construction documents after it receives and accepts the application for the Designed to Earn the ENERGY STAR program. *Image courtesy of U.S. Environmental Protection Agency.*

been reported and actual energy use assessed. The ENERGY STAR is awarded for the year for which it is applied; reapplication is required for subsequent years. The Designed to Earn the ENERGY STAR is awarded to construction documents that meet design targets for energy use. Buildings constructed from documents that earned the Designed to Earn the ENERGY STAR do not automatically qualify for the ENERGY STAR.

When a building constructed from documents that were awarded the Designed to Earn the ENERGY STAR applies for and receives the ENERGY STAR after a year of occupancy, a comparison between how a building was designed to perform and its actual performance becomes available. Designers, owners, and others can learn valuable information from any differences between the energy use targets (how the building was expected to perform based on its design) and actual energy use. Should the building not perform as expected, designers can apply lessons learned to future projects, and the owner will know to address any shortcomings through commissioning or other measures.

The ENERGY STAR rating considers source energy in its evaluation of energy use intensity. Source energy includes all raw fuel required to operate the building, including transmission, delivery, and production losses. By factoring source energy into its calculations—rather than site energy, which is the amount of energy consumed as reflected in utility bills—the total energy consumed in a building is accounted for, resulting in a common unit for equitable benchmarking among buildings with different energy sources.

ELIGIBILITY

The ENERGY STAR program is open only to buildings in the United States, where more than half the commercial floor space is eligible to earn the ENERGY STAR and the Designed to Earn the ENERGY STAR.[1] Buildings that typically qualify have more than 50 percent of gross floor area (excluding garage area) in the following building space type categories: bank branches, courthouses, dormitories, financial centers, hospitals, hotels, K-12 schools, medical offices, offices, religious worship facilities, retail stores, supermarkets, and warehouses. The remaining 50 percent of gross floor area may be occupied by any of the space types just listed or by one of these types: computer data center, parking, swimming pool, and "other," with the following exceptions:

- The gross floor area (which excludes parking areas) must be greater than the combined floor area of all parking structures, enclosed or not.
- The combined floor area for all computer data center uses must not exceed 10 percent of the gross floor area.

- The combined floor area of spaces designated as "other" must not exceed 10 percent of the gross floor area.

- Where the primary space type is hospital, the only other space types that may be entered are computer data center, "other," parking, and swimming pool.

Criteria for Rating Building Energy Performance: Operating Characteristics

Where applicable, minimum and maximum thresholds by space type are shown in Tables 8-1 through 8-3. Operating characteristics for rating building energy performance have these minimum and maximum thresholds for eligibility to ensure similar operation with the peer group against which the building will be benchmarked.

DESIGNED TO EARN THE ENERGY STAR

The Designed to Earn the ENERGY STAR process is a straightforward way for a project team to establish and work toward energy efficiency goals. By engaging in the process, an owner is made aware of the potential financial benefits of energy conservation measures on operating costs and can make informed judgments about up-front expenditures.

A whole-building simulation for energy use is required, for which the time and expense will vary depending on the proposed building. There is no charge to use the ENERGY STAR tools or apply for the label, and the required paperwork is minimal and uncomplicated.

TABLE 8-1 MINIMUM AND MAXIMUM THRESHOLD VALUES FOR OFFICES, BANKS AND FINANCIAL INSTITUTIONS, COURTHOUSES, AND MEDICAL OFFICES

	Office	Bank/Financial	Courthouse	Medical Office
Gross Floor Area (ft²)	≥5,000	≥1,000	≥5,000	≥5,000
Operating Hours (Hrs/Weekly)	30 ≤ H/W ≤ 168	30 ≤ H/W ≤ 168	30 ≤ H/W ≤ 168	30 ≤ H/W ≤ 168
Personal Computers/ Registers (#)	# PCs ≥ 1	# PCs ≥ 1	# PCs ≥ 1	N/A
Workers on Main Shift/Seating Capacity (#)	≥1	≥1	≥1	≥1

Source: ENERGY STAR Summary Table, "Criteria for Rating Building Energy Performance: Operating Characteristics." Information has been reformatted and is reprinted with permission.

TABLE 8-2 MINIMUM AND MAXIMUM THRESHOLD VALUES FOR SUPERMARKETS, WAREHOUSES, RETAIL, AND K-12 SCHOOLS

	Supermarket	Refrigerated/ Nonrefrigerated Warehouse	Retail	K-12 School
Gross Floor Area (ft²)	≥5,000	≥5,000	≥5,000	≥5,000
Operating Hours (Hrs/Weekly)	30 ≤ H/W ≤ 168	30 ≤ H/W ≤ 168	30 ≤ H/W ≤ 168	N/A
Personal Computers/ Registers (#)	N/A	N/A	≥ 0 PCs, ≥ 1 register	# PCs ≥ 0
Workers on Main Shift/Seating Capacity (#)	≥1	≥1	≥1	N/A
Walk-in Refrigeration/ Freezer Units (#)	N/A	≥0	≥0	≥0
Open and Closed Refrigeration/ Freezer Cases (#)	N/A	N/A	≥0	N/A

Source: ENERGY STAR Summary Table, "Criteria for Rating Building Energy Performance: Operating Characteristics." Information has been reformatted and is reprinted with permission.

The Designed to Earn the ENERGY STAR program does not, however, assess water use, materials and resources, sustainable sites, and other nonenergy categories which are incorporated in the LEED-NC and Green Globes New Construction rating systems. Should a building be designed to achieve certification for one of these rating systems, it may also qualify for Designed

TABLE 8-3 MINIMUM AND MAXIMUM THRESHOLD VALUES FOR HOSPITALS, HOTELS, AND RESIDENCE HALLS AND DORMITORIES

	Hospital	Hotel	Residence Hall/Dormitory
Gross Floor Area (ft²)	20,000 ≤ ft² ≤ 5,000,000	≥5,000	≥5,000
Operating Hours (Hrs/Weekly)	30 ≤ H/W ≤ 168	N/A	30 ≤ H/W ≤ 168
Workers on Main Shift/ Seating Capacity (#)	N/A	≥1	≥1
Licensed Beds (#)	16 ≤ # beds ≤ 1,510	N/A	N/A
Rooms (#)	N/A	≥1	≥5
Floors (#)	1 ≤ # floors ≤ 40	N/A	N/A
Commercial Refrigeration/ Freezer Units (#)	N/A	≥0	N/A

Source: ENERGY STAR Summary Table, "Criteria for Rating Building Energy Performance: Operating Characteristics." Information has been reformatted and is reprinted with permission.

to Earn the ENERGY STAR without much additional cost or effort. By setting an energy target that is benchmarked against the actual energy performance of existing buildings, performance-based ENERGY STAR can complement LEED. Green Globes incorporates ENERGY STAR's Target Finder (described later in this chapter) into its New Construction program.

The Process

The application process for the Designed to Earn the ENERGY STAR is estimated to take about 20 minutes. To have the information needed to apply, however, an energy model of the building must be completed. There is no application fee. The design process for earning the Designed to Earn the ENERGY STAR is illustrated in Figure 8-3. The steps for applying for recognition are as follows:[2]

DESIGN PROCESS USING ENERGY STAR

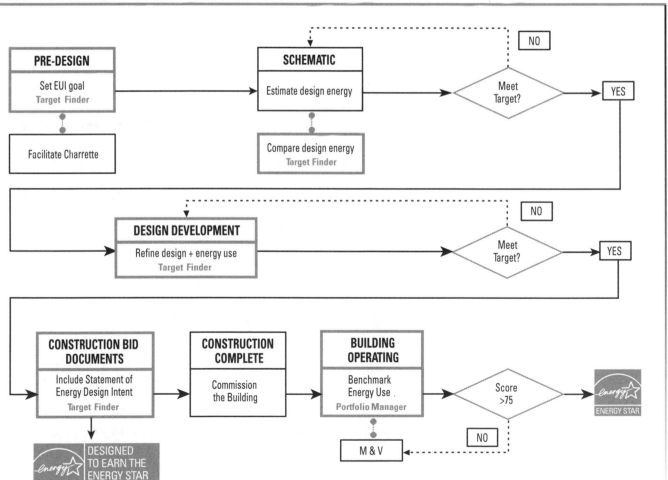

Figure 8-3 Flowchart of the design process using ENERGY STAR. *Image courtesy of U.S. Environmental Protection Agency.*

1. Determine the building design's energy performance rating. To be eligible to achieve Designed to Earn the ENERGY STAR, the design must attain an EPA energy performance rating of 75 or higher. This rating is determined through the Target Finder tool available on the ENERGY STAR website (described later in the chapter). Target Finder generates a Statement of Energy Design Intent.

2. Submit the project to the EPA after the construction documents are 95 percent complete but before the building is finished and generating utility bills. The architect of record must mail the Statement of Energy Design Intent with a completed application letter (also available online) to the EPA. The architect of record must be an ENERGY STAR Partner.

3. Within 10 days of receiving the application, the EPA will notify the architect of record whether the documents have been accepted. If they have been, the EPA will email the Designed to Earn the ENERGY STAR (shown in Figure 8-2) to the architect for inclusion on the construction documents.

ENERGY STAR Partners

Commercial building owners, constructors, and designers are among those eligible to join ENERGY STAR as a Partner. Partners are listed on the ENERGY STAR website; may use the ENERGY STAR logo to publicize their participation, as permitted in the partnership agreement; and may participate in ENERGY STAR awards and other recognition programs. Service providers are eligible for partnership if they submit commercial building designs for new construction that achieve the ENERGY STAR. To be eligible for existing construction, every 12 months service providers must provide at least 10 benchmarks by entering energy data into Portfolio Manager (described later in the chapter). Owners commit to benchmarking building energy performance, developing and implementing a plan to improve energy performance, and educating their staff and the public about their achievements with ENERGY STAR.

Target Finder

Although the Designed to Earn the ENERGY STAR is awarded near the end of the design process or during construction, the EPA recommends that the design team set an energy performance goal as early in the design process as possible. The Target Finder tool benchmarks the energy use intensity of a proposed building to that of a group of operating buildings in the DOE's

Commercial Building Energy Consumption Survey (CBECS) database that are similar in terms of climate and program.

Target Finder is available on the ENERGY STAR website (www. energystar.gov) as a one-page form which a design team member fills in with project data, including the zip code (to locate the climate zone), facility characteristics, and estimated design energy. (Eligible space types and operating characteristics were described earlier in this chapter.)

For each space type selected, users fill in such project characteristics as gross square feet; hours of operation; number of workers, PCs, cash registers, and refrigerator and freezer units; and the percentage of floor area heated and/or cooled. Users can then identify the target rating they are seeking to achieve on a scale of 1 to 100, with 75 being the minimum rating eligible to receive the Designed to Earn the ENERGY STAR. An energy reduction target in percentages can be selected in lieu of a number—a useful option for major renovations. At this point, Target Finder can estimate target energy performance results based on the target, giving data on estimated annual energy use (in kBTUs), energy cost, and CO_2 emissions. The targeted energy use can give the project team a goal to work toward, or an "energy budget" for the building.

The data generated by Target Finder will include assumptions about the project's fuel mix, which can have a significant impact on the estimated energy performance. Once the design is complete and Target Finder has been used to produce documentation for the Designed to Earn the ENERGY STAR application, the user must input energy sources (electricity is a mandatory field), estimating total energy use from energy modeling and inputting the energy rate in dollars per unit. If the project includes on-site renewable energy generation, the estimated energy produced should be subtracted from the total energy used input in Target Finder—that is, Target Finder design energy estimates should include only the energy that is to be purchased from utility companies. Once total projected energy use data has been entered, Target Finder rates the design and compares estimated use data to the targeted energy use. Energy cost savings and carbon dioxide emission reductions are generated as well.

ENERGY STAR FOR COMMERCIAL BUILDINGS

For a building to earn an ENERGY STAR, it must be of an eligible building type; achieve an energy rating of 75 or higher; and have documentation, including certification by a professional engineer, approved by the EPA. The EPA estimates the time required to complete the initial benchmarking at one to two-and-a-half hours, including data collection and input into Portfolio Manager, a free Internet-based tool described later in this chapter. Once the initial benchmarking in Portfolio Manager is completed, the EPA estimates it will take less than five minutes per month to enter updates. The total time to complete the paperwork necessary to apply for the ENERGY STAR is estimated to be six hours, including collecting and inputting energy data and the engineer's time. The EPA charges no fee for applying for the ENERGY STAR for buildings.[3]

Energy Rating

For each building eligible for the ENERGY STAR—including those with designs that received the Designed to Earn the ENERGY STAR—12 consecutive months of actual energy use data from utility bills generated while the building was occupied must be submitted on Portfolio Manager for comparison with the energy use of similar buildings in the CBECS database. Buildings receiving 75 or more points out of 100 may receive a label for that year. A rating of 75 indicates the building is more energy efficient than 75 percent of similar buildings, while a score of 50 indicates average performance. Energy performance data for subsequent 12-month periods must be recorded on Portfolio Manager to be eligible for an ENERGY STAR in subsequent years.

The Process

To receive the ENERGY STAR, a Statement of Energy Performance (SEP) for the building must be generated by the Portfolio Manager tool, stamped or sealed by a professional engineer, and mailed to the EPA with a Letter of Agreement. The postmark on the application mailing must be within 120 days of the period ending date for the year of energy consumption used in determining the rating. Once the EPA has reviewed and approved the submitted materials, it will issue an ENERGY STAR plaque for the building for that year.

On the SEP, the engineer must certify that:

■ Indoor air pollutants are controlled, and adequate ventilation is provided, per ASHRAE Standard 62.

■ Thermal conditions meet ASHRAE Standard 55 requirements.

■ Adequate illumination is provided per IESNA Lighting Handbook for lighting quality.

The intent of this certification is to safeguard against energy-efficiency priorities compromising the quality of the indoor environment.

Portfolio Manager

Portfolio Manager is a Web-based tool that produces a rating of a building's actual energy performance from data the owner or manager inputs from 12 months of utility bills. The rating is benchmarked against the CBECS database of similar buildings to produce a score of up to 100 points; a minimum of 75 points is required to qualify for the ENERGY STAR. Space types, operation schedule, building area, and other project characteristics are taken into account in the energy rating. Water usage and cost data are also tracked.

In addition to benchmarking building performance against similar buildings, the tool benchmarks a building's performance against its own performance in past years, potentially identifying problem areas and identifying cost-effective areas to invest in improvements. It is also possible to track energy and water use in building types that are not eligible for the ENERGY STAR. For example, a city could use Portfolio Manager to benchmark energy use for all its public libraries against one another, even though "library" is not an eligible space type for the ENERGY STAR. The city could then use this data to set targets for energy use when planning improvements to an existing building or for a new facility.

Portfolio Manager can be used for one building or a group of buildings owned or managed by the same entity. A sharing feature allows the primary account holder to grant access to multiple users so they can modify data. A campus feature within Portfolio Manager allows energy managers of higher education and university campuses, office parks, and strip malls or retail campuses to track energy consumption from either multiple-facility or separate meters. The tool also can be used to apply for the ENERGY STAR for a single building or for multiple buildings at the same time.

CASE STUDY 1

Peloton Cycles, Fort Collins, Colorado

Figure 8-4 Part of the roof is made with structural insulated panels (SIPs), contributing to the high R-value of the building envelope. © 2009, Architecture West, LLC.

Climate: Cold (Zone 6)

Space Type: Retail

Size: 14,087 gross square feet

Completion Date: 2008

Target Finder Score: 99

Energy Use Intensity: 21.1 kBtu/square foot/year

Owner: Peloton Cycles, Loveland, Colorado

Architect: Architecture West, LLC, Fort Collins, Colorado

Structural Engineer: Weeks and Associates, Fort Collins, Colorado

Mechanical, Electrical, and Plumbing Engineer: SRB Consulting Engineering, Loveland, Colorado

Civil Engineer: JLB Engineering Consultants, Louisville, Colorado

Planner/Landscape Architect: The Frederickson Group LLC, Loveland, Colorado

General Contractor: Alliance Design Build Solutions, LLC, Loveland, Colorado

Figure 8-5 Over 90 percent of regularly occupied spaces receive natural daylight. © *2009, Architecture West, LLC.*

The Peloton Cycles building is on an 11,138-square-foot footprint with a 2,949-square-foot mezzanine level. Peloton Cycles occupies 11,969 square feet, and there is a 2,118-square-foot tenant space. It is expected that the project will receive LEED-CS Gold certification.

Figure 8-6 Two-stage infrared tube heaters provide primary heat for the building. © 2009, Architecture West, LLC.

Energy-Saving Features

BUILDING ENVELOPE

The building envelope has high R-values, with part of the roof made of structural insulated panels (SIPs). Over 90 percent of the regularly occupied spaces have sufficient daylighting to perform normal tasks without artificial lighting.

MECHANICAL SYSTEM

The building is primarily heated by two-stage infrared tube heaters (see Figure 8-6) that are rated at 93 percent efficiency. The mezzanine level is heated with high-efficiency gas-fired units. Outdoor air is provided through a heat recovery ventilator, coupled with a gas-fired duct heater rated at 90 percent efficiency. The direct evaporative cooling system offers significant energy savings over a compressor air conditioning unit.

Tips from the Architect

Regarding the Designed to Earn the ENERGY STAR program, Architecture West, LLC's Chris Yates, LEED AP, says that a benefit of the program is that ENERGY STAR is a widely recognized symbol that lets owners display their commitment to the environment to their clientele. Yates adds, "It validates the architectural design for our present and future clientele." However, he cautions, "It is not a design tool. You plug your building in and get out an answer. The Target Finder system will not help you determine how to improve your building or your score."[4]

Figure 8-7 The new T.C. Williams High School was built immediately adjacent to the existing school, which continued to be occupied during construction and was later demolished. *Image © 2007, Judy Davis/HDPhoto. Courtesy of Hoachlander Davis Photography, LLC.*

Climate: Hot-Mixed(Zone 4)

Space Type: K–12 school

Size: 461,000 gross square feet

Completion Date: 2007

Construction Cost: $80 million

Target Finder Score: 75

Energy Use Intensity: 112 kBtu/square feet/year

Annual Energy Savings (Projected): 16,093.839 kBtu

Annual Carbon Savings (Projected): 2,882,600 pounds

Owner: Alexandria City Public Schools

Architect: Moseley Architects, Richmond, Virginia

Structural Engineer: Moseley Architects, Richmond, Virginia

Mechanical, Electrical, and Plumbing Engineer: Moseley Architects, Richmond, Virginia

Civil Engineer: ADTEK Engineers, Fairfax, Virginia

Constructor: Hansel Phelps Construction Company, Chantilly, Virginia

Figure 8-8 About 10,000 square feet of the roof is extensively planted. *Image © 2007, Judy Davis/HDPhoto. Courtesy of Hoachlander Davis Photography, LLC.*

Built immediately adjacent to the building it replaced, the new T.C. Williams High School serves grades 10 through 12. In addition to providing more space for an expanding population, the new school design incorporated sustainable features, many of which may be integrated into the curriculum. Originally designed to achieve LEED-NC Gold, the team decided to also

Figure 8-9 Each cell of the cooling tower has a variable-speed fan, resulting in energy savings over traditional constant speed fan operation. *Image © 2007, Moseley Architects.*

pursue Designed to Earn the ENERGY STAR after energy modeling was completed.

Energy-Saving Features

BUILDING ENVELOPE

About 10,000 square feet of the roof is extensively planted. The balance has a high solar reflectance index (SRI), with the exception of a black strip of roofing included for educational purposes. Thermometers on each color segment of roofing illustrate the difference in temperature. Exterior glazing is high-perform-ance insulated glass with low-e coating.

MECHANICAL SYSTEM

The mechanical system includes enthalpy wheels in air handlers, variable-primary pumping for chilled water and hot water, variable-air volume air deliv-ery, carbon dioxide sensors to indicate occupancy levels, high-efficiency condensing boilers, and best-efficiency control sequences. A building automa-tion system measures and tracks water and energy use and makes this informa-tion available for use in the school curriculum.

TIPS FROM THE ARCHITECT

This is the first project Moseley Architects undertook with the Designed to Earn the ENERGY STAR program, and the firm is considering participating with other projects. "Target Finder is a good tool," said Director of Environmental Planning and Research Bryna Dunn, AICP, LEED AP. "It gives the engineer an energy budget, in addition to a money budget." Dunn emphasized the importance of inputting as accurate information as possible into the Target Finder, noting that a small change can have a big impact on the rating.[5]

CASE STUDY 3

Hess Tower, Houston, Texas

Figure 8-10 This 30-story office tower is located in a new park in downtown Houston. The first two floors of the tower are lobby and retail space, with 28 floors of Class A office space above. In addition to the Designed to Earn the ENERGY STAR label, the project is expected to be certified at the LEED Gold level. *Image property of Gensler.*

Climate: Hot-Humid (Zone 2)

Space Type: Office

Size: 948,000 gross square feet

Completion Date: 2010

Estimated Construction Cost: Not available

Target Finder Score: 99

Energy Use Intensity: 36 kBTU/square feet/year

Annual Energy Savings (Projected): 12,915,000 kBTU, $294,000

Annual Carbon Savings (Projected): 2,382 pounds

Owner: Trammell Crow Company/CBRE, Houston, Texas

Architect: Gensler, Houston, Texas

Structural Engineer: Haynes Whaley & Associates, Houston, Texas

Mechanical, Electrical, and Plumbing Engineer: Wylie Consulting
  Engineers, Houston, Texas

Civil Engineer: Walter P. Moore, Houston, Texas

Landscape Architect: Office of James Burnett, Houston, Texas

Lighting Consultant: Archiluce International, Atlanta, Georgia

Constructor: Gilbane Building Company, Houston, Texas

This 30-story office tower is located in a new 12-acre park in downtown Houston. Hess Tower's plaza is intended to blend seamlessly with the park, contributing to a pedestrian-friendly district. The first two floors of the tower are lobby and retail space, with 28 floors of Class A office space above. In addition to the Designed to Earn the ENERGY STAR, the project is precertified at the LEED Gold level.

Figure 8-11 Wind turbines at the top of the Discovery Tower are a visible reminder of the building's sustainable building program. *Image property of Gensler.*

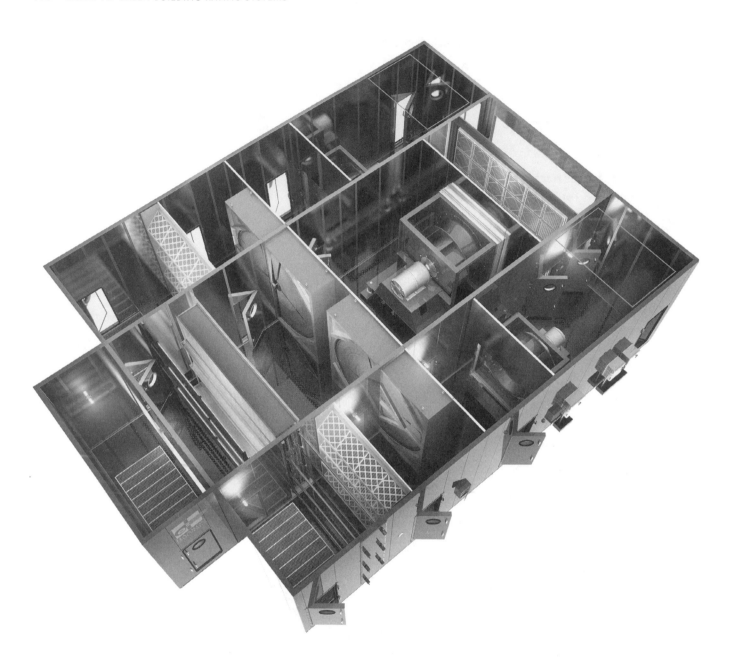

Figure 8-12 The two energy recovery wheels in the middle of this custom energy recovery unit pretreat outside air by removing moisture and transferring it to the exhaust airstream. Dual wheels transfer the maximum amount of heat between the building's exhaust/relief air and the fresh air entering the building. *Image © 2008, Bernard Seo, Dreamscape Creations. Courtesy of Haakon Industries.*

Developer Trammell Crow's project manager Adam Saphier, LEED AP, is pleased the building will have a smaller environmental footprint, but says the decision was market-driven. "We and our partners said, 'Let's make this the most healthy, productive, and comfortable office building in Houston.'" Although the wind turbines will generate less than 1 percent of the building's electricity, Saphier says the turbines are a visible symbol of the building's commitment to sustainability. "Houston is the energy capital of the world, and it's turning into what could be the alternative energy capital of the world," says Saphier.[6]

Energy-Saving Features

BUILDING ENVELOPE

Advanced high-performance, low-e glazing with external solar shading on the south elevation reduces the cooling load. The roof has a high solar reflectance index rating and high insulation R-value. A vegetated roof covers the entry pavilion.

MECHANICAL SYSTEM

The highly efficient HVAC system includes an energy recovery wheel and high-performance chillers. Air monitoring and increased ventilation contribute to improved indoor air quality.

RENEWABLE ENERGY

Energy produced by wind turbines at the top of the building is harvested and fed into the building's electrical system, reducing the electrical load by about 100,000 kWh per year.

RESOURCES

Refer to these pages on the ENERGY STAR website:

www.energystar.gov/newbuildingdesign: Here you'll find links to numerous resources, including:

- Building design guidelines recommending tasks for each phase of design, as well as post-occupancy measurement and verification to help the design team reach its energy efficiency goals
- The Target Finder tool and answers to frequently asked questions about Target Finder
- A Designed to Earn the ENERGY STAR page, including online training for architects and a downloadable Building Energy Performance Specification with boilerplate language to modify for inclusion in a request for proposal, contract, or specifications

www.energystar.gov/benchmark: This page contains details about Portfolio Manager, including links to these resources:

- The ENERGY STAR Benchmarking Starter Kit, featuring a data collection worksheet and animated training guide
- The "Professional Engineer's Guide to the ENERGY STAR Label for Commercial Buildings," a 32-page document describing the expecta-

tions, and limitations, of the professional engineer's role in confirming the accuracy of data entered into Portfolio Manager and in verifying that indoor environment criteria are met

■ Reference energy performance targets for commercial building types that are currently ineligible to receive a rating

■ Sample Statement of Energy Performance

■ The Portfolio Manager Tour, a tutorial in using the software tool

www.energystar.gov: From the ENERGY STAR homepage follow the Tools and Resources Library link from the Buildings and Plants section to many tools for creating an effective energy management plan, including spreadsheets and information on improving building performance.

www.energystar.gov/training: Under Buildings and Plants take the link to live and pre-recorded training sessions on a range of ENERGY STAR topics.

NOTES

1. Excerpted from "Criteria for Rating Building Energy Performance," www.energystar. gov/index.cfm?c=eligibility.bus_portfoliomanager_eligibility; supplemented by information from Karen Butler, U.S. EPA Manager for ENERGY STAR Commercial New Construction, telephone conversation with the author, July 31, 2008.

2. Karen Butler, U.S. EPA, telephone conversation with the author, July 31, 2008; and "Achieving Designed to Earn the ENERGY STAR," www.energystar.gov/ index.cfm?c=new_bldg_design.new_bldg_design_benefits.

3. Time estimates from Karen Butler, U.S. EPA, conversation with the author, July 31, 2008.

4. Chris Yates, LEED AP, Architecture West, LLC, email to the author, August 5, 2008.

5. Bryna Dunn, AICP, LEED AP, Director of Environmental Planning and Research for Moseley Architects, Richmond, Virginia, telephone conversation with the author, July 31, 2008.

6. Adam Saphier, LEED AP, Project Manager, Trammell Crow, telephone conversation with the author, August 4, 2008.

9

GREEN GLOBES

The Green Globes® rating system was first developed in Canada by ECD Energy and Environment using the United Kingdom's BRE Environmental Assessment Method (BREEAM) as a starting point. The development process for new construction began in 1996, and what is now known as Green Globes was completed in 2002. Green Globes for Existing Buildings was adopted in 2004 by the Building Owners and Manufacturers Association of Canada, where it is now known as *Go GreenPlus.* Green Globes came to the United States in 2004 when the nonprofit organization Green Building Initiative® (GBI) acquired the license to promote and develop Green Globes in the United States. Since 2004, the development of Green Globes in the United States (the focus of this chapter) for both new and existing construction has been independent from the development of Green Globes based programs in Canada.[1]

Commercial and multifamily residential buildings can earn up to 1,000 points in 7 categories. In descending order of weight, they are: Energy (300 points); Indoor Environment (160 points); Resources/Materials (145 points); Water (130 points); Site (120 points); Project Management (100 points); and Emissions (45 points). Four levels of certification are available: one globe for achieving 35 to 54 percent of available points; two globes for 55 to 69 percent of available points; three globes for 70 to 84 percent of available points; and four globes for 85 to 100 percent of available points. Levels are determined by percentages rather than flat point totals to reflect that the total number of points varies by project; that is, although 1,000 points are available, points that cannot be earned because of project specifics are deducted from

Figure 9-1 An example of the aluminum plaque indicating Green Globes certification. Four Green Globes, the highest level of achievement, were awarded to an existing office building in Portland, Oregon. *Photo courtesy of Green Building Initiative.*

that total number. For example, if local codes do not allow for on-site treatment of wastewater, then the total number of points available will be reduced by the number of points allocated to a graywater system.

The GBI sees as its primary market for Green Globes the mainstream builders, designers, and developers for whom green building is not a significant part of their practice and seeks to offer an alternative assessment and rating system that is cost-effective.[2] Users complete an online survey for every category at each of eight stages of design and construction. The software tool tracks scoring as the project progresses and suggests ways to increase the score. As of mid-2009 the GBI had certified 30 new buildings and 38 existing buildings; 2,300 other buildings had been registered.[3]

ELIGIBILITY

Commercial and institutional buildings of any size and multifamily residential buildings more than three stories in height may apply for certification. There is a Green Globes rating system for new construction (NC) which includes major renovations, and for existing buildings, called Continual Improvement of Existing Buildings (CIEB). To be eligible for Green Globes certification for new construction, users must:

1. Buy a subscription from the GBI website.
2. Complete the project questionnaire, using the online tools.

3. Earn at least 35 percent of available points.

4. Receive a third-party assessment at two stages of design and construction.

GREEN GLOBES: THE ANSI STANDARD

In 2005, the GBI became accredited as a standards developer by the American National Standards Institute (ANSI) and began the process of establishing Green Globes as an ANSI standard,[4] GBI 01-200XP: Green Building Assessment Protocol for Commercial Buildings. The name of the approved standard will be Green Globes v. 2.[5] The process is scheduled to be completed for New Construction in early 2010, at which time the ANSI process for Green Globes for Continuous Improvement of Existing Buildings CIEB is expected to begin.[6]

The NC rating system is expected to be revised as follows:[7]

■ Minimum point thresholds for each category will be introduced. Table 9-1 lists the proposed minimums.

■ The number of points available for life-cycle assessment (LCA) will be increased.

■ The EcoCalculator, an online LCA tool, will be incorporated into the standard.

■ A water consumption calculator will be added to the online tools for use with the standard.

TABLE 9-1 PROPOSED POINT MINIMUMS

Environmental Assessment Area	Total Points Available	Minimum Percentage of Points Required for Compliance at Each of the Four Levels
Project Management	100	50%
Site	120	24% (0 for major renovations)
Energy	300	Performance Path A: 50% Prescriptive Path B: 33%
Water*	130	26%
Resources/Materials	145	29%
Emissions	45	9%
Indoor Environment	160	32%
Total	1000 (less nonapplicable points)	

*The Water Assessment Area has a unique method for calculating final point calculations. Please refer to section 9.1 (of the Standard) for more information.

Source: Table 2, "GBI Proposed American National Standard 01-200XP: Green Building Assessment Protocol for Commercial Buildings." Public Review Draft, October 2, 2009. Provided by the Green Building Initiative. Reprinted with permission.

THE PROCESS

The GBI describes the process for receiving certification of new construction as follows:[8]

1. Purchase a subscription to Green Globes at www.thegbi.org. A free 30-day trial is available; information entered during the trial period will remain accessible if a subscription is purchased within 90 days of trial expiration.

2. Enter basic building information and complete the online questionnaire. The questionnaire is completed in eight stages: predesign-project initiation stage; predesign-site analysis; predesign-programming; schematic design; design development; construction documents; contracting and construction; and commissioning.

3. Based on the information entered at each stage, a rating score will be issued and feedback given through automatic reports. Feedback may include supplementary information or generic suggestions for improving building performance. The GBI describes the online tool as "a virtual green building consultant."[9] Note, a subscription must be purchased to receive a self-assessed score.

4. If the building scores a minimum of 35 percent on the self-assessment, it is likely to qualify for certification, so a Stage I third-party assessment should be scheduled. This assessment consists of a review of documentation. A Stage I assessment may take place as soon as construction documents are nearly complete and as late as almost one year after occupancy. After one year of occupancy, Green Globes CIEB should be used for certification. To fully realize the benefits of the NC assessment tool, the GBI recommends implementing it before construction begins.[10]

5. A Stage II third-party assessment can be scheduled at this time, and should take place after substantial completion but before occupancy. This assessment reviews additional documentation and includes an on-site walkthrough and interviews with project team members. A pre-assessment checklist is available online.

6. The Green Globes Rating and Certification is issued, usually in less than six weeks after the final assessment.[11]

THE COST

Fees required for certification are listed in Tables 9-2 and 9-3. Additional potential costs include those for energy simulations, implementing some of the credits and the time to document credits, which will vary by project and project

TABLE 9-2 FEES FOR NEW CONSTRUCTION(1)

Software Subscriptions Single Assessment/Certification Use (5 Year Subscription)					$500 per building	
Third Party Assessment/Certification Price per building based on building square footage (enclosed or occupied)						
Type of Third Party Assessment Service	<100,000 SF	100,000 to <200,000 SF	200,000 to <300,000 SF	300,000 to <400,000 SF	400,000 to <500,000 SF	>500,000 SF
NC Stage I(1)	$3,500	$4,000	$4,500	$5,500	$6,500	$7,500
NC Stage II(1)						
Complete NC Stage I and NC Stage II(1)	$7,000	$8,000	$9,000	$11,000	$13,000	$15,000
Assessor Travel Expenses(1)	$1,000 upfront flat fee or actual expenses plus 20 percent overhead billed after the assessment is completed (mandatory for all on-site assessments)(4)					
Multiple Space Types/ Complexity(2)	$1,500–$3,500					
Custom Energy Analysis(2)	$1,500–$3,500					
Expediting Fee(3)	$2,500 regardless of square footage					

(1) Purchase of a Green Globes software subscription, NC Stage I, and NC Stage II third party assessments, and Assessor travel expenses are all required to obtain a Green Globes rating/certification.

(2) Applicable for certain non-ENERGY STAR building types requiring custom energy analysis and other complex buildings that depart substantially from a standard office building. GBI will identify if this is applicable and the amount in advance of scheduling/performing third party assessment/certification services.

(3) Applicable if customer requests and GBI performs certification within less than four weeks from order/payment.

(4) Buildings located outside continental 48 states (Alaska, Hawaii, or U.S. territories) must select to pay actual expenses plus 20 percent for Assessor travel expenses (flat rate may not be used).

From Green Globes 2010 Price List. Reprinted with permission.

team. As with any rating system, there will likely be a learning curve while project team members familiarize themselves with Green Globes and its requirements. All reference materials are available online at no additional charge.

An example of registered buildings that required custom services are Veterans Affairs hospitals, which have many diverse space types—cafeteria, dedicated laundry, operating rooms, patient rooms, and so forth—requiring custom energy analysis.[12]

THIRD-PARTY VERIFICATION

Two stages of third-party verification are required under Green Globes for new construction. The first-stage assessment occurs at the end of the design phase when the questionnaire is completed and, ideally, before construction begins. It consists of a review of construction documents, management records, energy analysis, and other documentation. A pre-assessment checklist lists more than 100 documents, although the number will vary depending on which points are pursued. The assessor checks to be sure the

TABLE 9-3 FEES FOR EXISTING BUILDINGS(1)

Software Subscriptions					Price Each	
Annual Subscription (Single Assessment/Certification Use)(1)					$1,000 per building	
CIEB Pilot Portfolio Subscription Discount(2)					$2,000 per portfolio	
Third Party Assessment/Certification Price per building based on building square footage (enclosed or occupied)						
Type of Third Party Assessment Service	<100,000 SF	100,000 to <200,000 SF	200,000 to <300,000 SF	300,000 to <400,000 SF	400,000 to <500,000 SF	>500,000 SF
CIEB(1)	$4,000	$5,000	$6,000	$8,000	$10,000	$11,000
CIEB (Re-Certification)(1)	$3,500	$4,000	$4,500	$5,500	$6,500	$7,500
Assessor Travel Expenses(1)	$1,000 upfront flat fee or actual expenses +20% overhead billed after the assessment is completed (Mandatory for all on-site assessments)					
Multiple Space Types/ Complexity(3)	$1,000–$3,500					
Custom/Energy Analysis(3)	$1,000–$3,500					
Expediting Fee(4)	$2,500 regardless of square footage					

(1) Purchase of a Green Globes CIEB software subscription, CIEB third party assessment, and Assessor travel expenses are all required to obtain a Green Globes rating/certification.

(2) When a single organization purchases 20 or more CIEB building subscriptions in a single transaction, GBI will discount $2,000 from the total amount payable and due. Exclusive discount. One time use per organization.

(3) Applicable for highly complex, multiple space type buildings that depart substantially from a standard office building complexity and for certain non-ENERGY STAR building types requiring custom energy analysis. GBI will identify if this is applicable and the exact amount in advance of scheduling or performing services.

(4) Applicable if customer requests and GBI performs certification within less than four weeks from order/payment.

(5) Buildings located outside continental 48 states (Alaska, Hawaii, or U.S. territories) must select to pay actual expenses plus 20 percent for Assessor travel expenses (flat rate may not be used).

From Green Globes 2010 Price List. Reprinted with permission.

percentage of points awarded by the completed questionnaire is supported by the documentation.

The second stage of assessment includes further documentation review and a site visit to walk through the building and interview team members. The assessor may make adjustments to the score to reflect what is found in the field and the documents. Only after the two stages of assessment are completed may the building receive certification. A pre-assessment checklist can be downloaded from www.thegbi.org/training/customertraining.asp.

Assessors are authorized and trained by the GBI and typically have 10 or more years' experience in a relevant profession. Assessors' work is subject to the approval of and audit by senior assessors.

CERTIFICATION CRITERIA

The criteria for Green Globes are available as an online questionnaire and for free printable download from the GBI website. There are no mandatory prerequisites. Minimum point thresholds for each category will be introduced with the release of the Green Globes Standard scheduled for early 2010; proposed minimums are listed in Table 9-1. The final rating or score is given as a percentage of the points that are applicable to the particular project. The proposed standard lists the following reasons for a criterion to be considered nonapplicable:[13]

1. If a criterion does not apply to the building type (e.g., if there are no oil-fired burners on-site, questions related to oil-fired burners would be designated nonapplicable).

2. If a code or regulation overrides, conflicts with, or otherwise prevents compliance with a criterion.

3. If a criterion conflicts with best practices based on regional climatic differences.

The following overview is from the Green Globes v. 2 draft.[14]

Project Management

This category includes an integrated design process, environmental purchasing, and commissioning. There are 100 points available. Credit is given for measures such as setting performance goals during predesign, providing environmental management during and after construction, and developing and implementing a commissioning plan.

Site

This category focuses on minimizing the impact of development on the site ecology. There are 120 points available. Credit is given for measures such as site selection in a previously developed area, controlling and minimizing stormwater runoff, and mitigating heat islands by shading impervious surfaces and using cool roof strategies.

Energy

This category concentrates on reducing energy demand, improving energy efficiency, and reducing carbon dioxide emissions. There are 300 points available for the Performance Design Option and 250 points available for the Prescriptive Design Option. Both paths require that the building design comply with ANSI/ASHRAE/IESNA Standard 90.1-2007 or the local energy code.

For the performance path, credit is awarded for items such as reducing the building carbon dioxide equivalent, passive demand reduction, and measurement and verification protocols. For the prescriptive path, points are awarded for meeting minimum requirements by climate zone for thermal resistance and thermal transmittance values for opaque elements of the building envelope and for thermal transmittance and Solar Heat Gain Coefficients for fenestration. Additional points are available for meeting prescriptive requirements for different HVAC equipment, as well as for daylighting, energy-efficient lighting measures, and renewable energy sources.

Water

This category addresses water conservation. There are 130 points available. Credit is given for meeting water performance targets, minimizing potable water consumption, and collecting rainwater. Some points are available depending on the specific building or building type—for example, whether there is a laundry operations or a cooling tower. A points calculation methodology normalizes available and awarded points to ensure that the minimum percentage of points required in this category is not skewed. A calculator tool is available online.

Resources/Materials

This category is concerned with low-impact materials; durability; minimizing waste from construction, renovation, and demolition; reusing existing structures; and controlling moisture There are 145 points available. The performance path offers 33 points, and the prescriptive path offers 25 points. The performance path uses the Green Globes LCA Credit Calculator for Building Assemblies to evaluate the structural system and building envelope during the conceptual design phase. The prescriptive path awards points for

Figure 9-2 This engineered lumber is made from composites of wood chips held together by adhesive made from wood bark instead of fossil fuels. This material meets some of the goals of the Resources/Materials category. *Photo by Warren Gretz. Courtesy of DOE/NREL.*

specifying materials that meet a particular percentage of recycled content or bio-based products. Points are also awarded for products and materials harvested, reclaimed, salvaged, extracted, processed, or manufactured within a 500-mile radius of the project site, or shipped primarily by water or rail within a 1,500-mile radius.

Emissions

This category is concerned with minimizing ozone depletion and pollution, and with preventing contamination of waterways and sewers. There are 45 points available. Credit is given for specifying low-NOx boilers and furnaces and refrigerant systems that don't use ozone-depleting substances. Other measures include preventing contaminants from entering sewers or waterways and implementing an integrated pest management plan.

Indoor Environment

This category focuses on effective ventilation; controlling indoor pollutants; and daylight, artificial light levels, and thermal and acoustic comfort. There are 160 points available. Credit is given for such items as providing ambient daylight to 80 percent of primary spaces, mitigating indoor pollution, and designing the ventilation system to avoid entraining pollutants into the ventilation path.

CASE STUDY 1

Duncan Avenue Community Center, University of Arkansas, Fayetteville, Arkansas

Figure 9-3 This community center serves the 200 students who live in the adjacent Duncan Avenue Apartments. The apartments are also Green Globes certified. *Photo courtesy Kent Perrodin, University Housing, University of Arkansas, Fayetteville.*

Climate: Mixed-Humid (Zone 4)

Size: 3,400 square feet, two stories

Construction Cost: Estimated $175.35 per square foot

Completion Date: 2009

Owner: University of Arkansas, Fayetteville, Arkansas

Architects: Allison Architects, Inc., Fayetteville, Arkansas, and Little Diversified Architectural Consulting, Charlotte, North Carolina

Mechanical/Electrical Engineer: TME Consulting Engineers, Fayetteville, Arkansas

Structural Engineer: FHA Consulting Engineers, Fayetteville, Arkansas

Constructor: Flintco, Springdale, Arkansas

Percentage Achieved: 63 percent, two globes

Duncan Avenue Community Center, Fayetteville, Arkansas Percentages Achieved (Two Globes)	
Project Management	90%
Site	72%
Energy	43%
Water	91%
Resources	80%
Emissions	74%
Indoor Environment	70%
Total Score	**63%**

The Duncan Avenue Community Center contains a fitness room, a small kitchenette, and a common room with a fireplace and television. It serves as the common area for the 200 students living in the Duncan Avenue Apartments nearby. The 50 apartments, divided into four three-story buildings, received a One Globe certification.

The University of Arkansas was the first higher education institution in the country to specify Green Globes as an option. Although the university's board of trustees allows certification by either LEED or Green Globes, the Green Building Initiative lobbied the school and offered free certification for the community center and the apartments.[15] The apartments were the first residential buildings certified by the GBI.

Figure 9-4 In addition to this common room, the community center also offers a fitness room and small kitchenette. *Photo courtesy Kent Perrodin, University Housing, University of Arkansas, Fayetteville.*

Sustainable Features

Sustainable features in the community center include energy-efficient mechanical equipment and artificial lighting. Stormwater runoff is controlled and minimized.

Tips from the Architect

"As a firm, our experience was with LEED," said Matthew Cabe, intern project architect at Allison Architects. Cabe, who handled Green Globes documentation and construction administration at the community center, said using Green Globes required some adjustment. He found Green Globes to be "not as onerous as LEED. It leaves more up to the professionals. It was very easy to work with; the online system was very user-friendly and did help with the planning and design process. The multiple stages kept issues at the forefront and helped the team stay focused."[16]

Tips from the Constructor

Kyle Cook, project manager for Flintco, said, "Our responsibility for Green Globes was fairly limited. It felt like any other project." Cook said the architect and university handled the Green Globes aspects, and he worked with the commissioning agent. From his perspective, no extra time was required to pursue Green Globes certification since commissioning is standard for University of Arkansas construction projects.

Cook's advice for other builders: "Have a preconstruction meeting with the commissioning agent and subcontractors to see what expectations are."[17]

Figure 9-5 This office and warehouse building is located adjacent to the Chandler Municipal Airport. The building received high marks for site design and enhancements which minimized its environmental impact. *Photo courtesy of Jack MacDonough.*

Climate: Hot-Dry (Zone 2)

Size: 30,000 square feet total: 3,000 square feet of office space and 27,000 square feet of warehouse space

Construction Cost: $4.8 million

Completion Date: 2008

Developer: Irgens Development Partners, LLC, Phoenix, Arizona

Design/Build Firm: Nagaki Design Build Associates Inc., Phoenix, Arizona

Mechanical Engineer: Mechanical Designs, Inc., Phoenix, Arizona

Electrical Engineer: Specified Electrical Contractors, Inc., Phoenix, Arizona

Structural Engineer: GFG Structural Engineers, Scottsdale, Arizona

Percentage Achieved: 41 percent, one Green Globe

Chandler Airport Commerce Center, Chandler, Arizona Percentages Achieved (One Green Globe)	
Project Management	54%
Site	72%
Energy	27%
Water	33%
Resources	35%
Emissions	56%
Indoor Environment	50%
Total Score	41%

"We pursued sustainable design and construction as part of our commitment to environmental responsibility," said Mark Irgens, president of Irgens Development Partners, LLC. "We chose to use the Green Globes system because of its ease of use and its ability to assist us in meeting our goals to reduce our impact on the environment and the surrounding community, and because it is user-friendly and affordable."[18]

Figure 9-6 The developer of this office and warehouse building also has a Green Globes certified medical office building in Illinois. *Photo courtesy of Jack MacDonough.*

Sustainable Features

Sustainable features include site design and development to minimize the environmental impact on the site, indoor air quality measures, an integrated design process, environmental purchasing, and commissioning.

Tips from the Architect

Larry Nagaki, LEED AP, principal, said this is the firm's first Green Globes building. He found Green Globes "fairly straightforward," adding, "Green

Globes takes a more practical stance than LEED. Its strength is the lack of bureaucracy." Nagaki said that warehouses are a difficult building type to certify—there is a large volume of space to condition, windows for daylighting are not desirable, there are not a lot of interior finishes to get credits for, and so forth.[19]

Tips from the Builder

"The earlier that you know you're going to go through the Green Globes process, the easier it will be," said Mike Derkenne, vice president of construction operations for Nelson Phoenix, LLC. In their case, construction was underway when they started pursuing Green Globes certification. "It worked out, but it would have been easier to have started with it," he said.

Comparing Green Globes to LEED, Derkenne found Green Globes to be easier and more user-friendly. From the construction side, "It [certification] didn't cost the project any additional money, other than time [spent] collecting more product data."[20]

CASE STUDY 3

Apple Valley Liquor Store No. 3, Apple Valley, Minnesota

Figure 9-7 The natural stone on the façade, Minnesota Greenolite, is from a quarry less than 250 miles from the building site. *Photo by Brian Droege. Courtesy of CNH Architects.*

Climate: Cold (Zone 6)

Size: 15,800 square feet, one story

Construction Cost: Estimated $200 per square foot

Completion Date: 2009

Owner: City of Apple Valley

Architect: CNH Architects, Inc., Apple Valley, Minnesota

Mechanical/Electrical Engineer: EDI, Ltd., Minneapolis, Minnesota

Structural Engineer: Van Sickle, Allen & Associates, Structural Engineers, Plymouth, Minnesota

Civil Engineer: Bonestroo, St. Paul, Minnesota

Landscape Architect: Damon Farber Associates, Minneapolis, Minnesota

Food Service Equipment: Robert Rippe and Associates, Minnetonka, Minnesota

General Contractor: Ebert Construction, Corcoran/Loretto, Minnesota

Percentage Achieved: 68, two Green Globes

Apple Valley Liquor Store No. 3, Apple Valley, Minnesota Percentages Achieved (Two Globes)	
Project Management	90%
Site	72%
Energy	63%
Water	38%
Resources	72%
Emissions	100%
Indoor Environment	75%
Total Score	**68%**

This municipal liquor store is mainly retail space but also includes a warehouse and staff offices supporting the retail function. The building is expected to use half the energy of a conventional retail building of the same size.

Figure 9-8 This bar is used for beer and wine tastings at store events. Store lighting is controlled for daylight harvesting. The carpet and vinyl tile adhesives are low-VOC. *Photo by Brian Droege. Courtesy of CNH Architects.*

Sustainable Features

The building is heated and cooled with a geothermal heat pump system, while a heat exchanger uses exhaust air to preheat or precool ventilation air. The building is projected to save $10,000 in its first year of operation. The building has no boilers, flue gasses, or other sources of air emission pollution, and no or low-VOC paints and adhesives were specified. Daylight harvesting strategies were employed, including dimming and occupancy sensors. Windows, clerestory windows, skylights, and solar tubes bring natural light to most retail and working areas of the building.

The roof is a white, reflective cool roof that mitigates the heat island effect. The structure is designed to support a living green roof at a future date, and the canopy is currently planted with a green roof. Site landscaping is drought-resistant and will not require irrigation once established. Stormwater is managed by catch basins and infiltration ponds that run into an existing on-site surge pond.

Figure 9-9 The Beer Cave is a walk-in cooler where shoppers can pick up cases of beer. The cooler is integrated with the geothermal heat pump system. *Photo by Brian Droege. Courtesy of CNH Architects.*

Tips from the Architect

Wayne Hilbert, AIA, LEED AP, principal at CNH Architects, says, "If you have a generally good handle on sustainable concepts, it is easy to pick up most of the Green Globes process without much effort. There are a few items that I find a bit quirky, and a few items that seem more appropriate in residential design, but the bulk of the system is very straightforward. The program is especially great for the medium to small projects, where cost and time are a big concern. It is also good for clients that want a green building, but are not real concerned with the final rating."

In terms of the strengths of Green Globes, Hilbert says, "I like the points for acoustical control, online surveys, quick certification process, simplified documentation requirements, on-site verification visit and cost. Also, Green Globes accepts more certified wood programs than just FSC." As to weaknesses, he notes that the survey questions are not always clear and points out that there is no flexibility to earn points for innovation.[21]

Green Globes versus LEED

Hilbert says, "If you understand green design concepts, Green Globes is easy to learn and start using at a one- to three-globe level. If you are pursuing a four-globe project, there would be some areas to learn that are different than other rating systems. Right now LEED has more and better learning opportunities." Hilbert also said that if you want to target a level for certification (for example, two globes), it is somewhat difficult to pinpoint what is required since the final score results from weighted percentages rather than points.

"I am a LEED AP, but I have not been able to convince one of my clients to pursue and pay for the LEED process. LEED has a more established infrastructure, which gives it better recognition and support in the industry. Vendors and product representatives are always selling their LEED benefits. Few even know of Green Globes. LEED also has better defined and understandable sustainable goals."[22]

Additional Costs

Regarding costs, Hilbert says, "The cost beyond a standard design project included the energy modeling fee, commissioning fee, and application fee to Green Globes. The team did not charge an additional fee for design or process time, which was minimal. The project surveys are generally quick and easy to fill out. The backup paperwork for verification is mostly information that is normally provided as part of the project. In the future, our design team may charge a small additional fee for handling the process, but not much."[23]

RESOURCES

Green Globes, www.thegbi.org: Tools such as the questionnaire (available for subscription or free trial), a pre-assessment checklist, and a life-cycle assessment (LCA) calculator are available here. The site also has a printable version of each phase of the assessment questionnaire available for free download, as well as project case studies and other resources. The LCA calculator allows design teams to compare different assembly choices for embodied energy, pollution, and global warming potential. Use of the GBI-commissioned Green Globes LCA Credit Calculator will be required in the Green Globes standard scheduled for release in 2010. A generic version of this software, the ATHENA® EcoCalculator for Assemblies, can be found at www.athenasmi.org/tools/ecoCalculator.

NOTES

1. Mark Rossolo, Director, State and Local Outreach, GBI, email to the author, June 29, 2009.
2. "Green Building Initiative Principles and Market Approach," www.thegbi.org/about-gbi/guiding-principles/position.asp; accessed June 5, 2009.
3. Rossolo, email to the author, July 22, 2009.
4. "History of the Green Globes System," www.thegbi.org/commercial/about-green-globes; accessed June 8, 2009.

5. Rossolo, email to the author, October 13, 2009.

6. Rossolo, emails to the author, June 20, 2009 and October 13, 2009.

7. Ibid.

8. "Green Globes Rating/Certification," http://thegbi.org/green-globes-tools/ratings-and-certifications.asp, unless otherwise noted; accessed June 5, 2009.

9. Rossolo, June 29, 2009.

10. Ibid.

11. Ibid.

12. Ibid., July 22, 2009.

13. "GBI Proposed American National Standard 01-200XP: Green Building Assessment Protocol for Commercial Buildings" Public Review Draft, October 2, 2009, p. 7. Reprinted with permission.

14. Ibid, pp. 1–102.

15. James Milner, Construction Coordinator, University of Arkansas Department of Facilities Management, email to the author, from Steve Voorhies, Manager of Media Relations, University of Arkansas, July 23, 2009.

16. Matthew Cabe, intern project architect, Allison Architects, telephone interview with the author, July 14, 2009.

17. Kyle Cook, Project Manager, Flintco, telephone interview with the author, July 16, 2009.

18. In July 31, 2009 email to the author sent by Angela Mork, Marketing Manager, Irgens Development, LLC.

19. Larry Nagaki, LEED AP, Principal, Nagaki Design Build Associates Inc., telephone interview with the author, July 24, 2009.

20. Mike Derkenne, Vice President of Construction Operations for Nelson Phoenix, LLC, telephone conversation with the author, July 29, 2009.

21. Wayne Hilbert, AIA, LEED AP, email to the author, August 24, 2009.

22. Ibid.

23. Ibid.

10

LEED FOR COMMERCIAL NEW CONSTRUCTION

EED® is a national rating system developed by the nonprofit U.S. Green Building Council (USGBC). LEED Version 1.0, which evolved into LEED for New Construction (LEED-NC), was launched in the United States in 1998 and grew to become the dominant green building assessment system for new construction there. It spread to other countries, with 161 projects certified in 91 countries by mid-2009.[1]

Following the success of LEED-NC, the USGBC developed rating systems for other building types, including the following systems for commercial construction: LEED Core and Shell Development (LEED-CS), Schools New Construction and Major Renovations (LEED for Schools), Existing Buildings: Operations and Maintenance (LEED-EB), and Commercial Interiors (LEED-CI). Additional commercial programs under development at this writing include LEED for Healthcare, LEED for Retail, and LEED for Retail Interiors.

Up to 110 points may be earned in 7 different categories: Sustainable Sites; Water Efficiency; Energy and Atmosphere; Materials and Resources; Indoor Environmental Quality; Innovation in Design; and Regional Priority. The number of points available in each category varies slightly depending on which system is being used, with indoor environmental quality receiving more weight in LEED for Schools. There are four different levels of certification:

Figure 10-1 The USGBC develops the LEED rating systems. *Image courtesy of the USGBC.*

Certified (40 to 49 points), Silver (50 to 59 points), Gold (60 to 79 points), and Platinum (80 or more points).

The initial version of LEED-NC has been modified several times. With the release of the LEED 2009 suite of rating systems came the following changes to previous versions of LEED:

- *Credit Weighting:* The total number of points available was increased to 100 base points plus 10 bonus points available for Innovation in Design and Regional Priority. Credit values were redistributed to align with environmental priorities to increase the weight of measures that limit or reduce climate change. The proportion of Sustainable Sites and Energy and Atmosphere points increased, whereas Materials and Resources credits now receive less weight than in previous versions.

- *Harmonization:* The prerequisites and credits across the five commercial rating systems in LEED 2009 have been aligned and harmonized to standardize the different rating systems.

- *Regionalization:* The four-credit Regional Priority category was added to provide bonus points for existing credits to address regionally specific environmental priorities. Green Building Council chapters and other local affiliates identified six credits to prioritize for each LEED 2009 rating system for regions of every state as identified by zip code.

- *LEED Online v3:* The online tool used by project teams to manage the project registration, documentation, and certification process has been upgraded. It includes access to LEED credit forms and links fields across credit forms. Credit Interpretation Rulings (CIRs) for LEED 2009 can be accessed, but CIRs issued for earlier versions of LEED have been scrubbed and the issues addressed in the LEED 2009 rating systems.

- *Introduction of Minimum Program Requirements:* These are listed in the next section and include a requirement that all certified projects with their own meters share energy and water usage data for at least five years of occupancy so that the USGBC can track actual building performance. This requirement remains in force even if the certified project changes ownership or tenancy. If this or other minimum program requirements are not met, certification may be revoked.

ELIGIBILITY

LEED-NC and LEED-CS may be earned by commercial, institutional, or high-rise residential building types. LEED for Schools must be used for any academic buildings on K-12 school grounds. Pre-K and postsecondary school buildings may qualify for LEED for Schools or LEED-NC. For LEED-NC, LEED-CS, and LEED for Schools, the project must include new design and construction or the major renovation of a building in its entirety. All prerequisites must be met and at least 40 optional credits must be earned. The process for certification, including registration, documentation of credits, and third-party verification, must be followed.[2]

For LEED-NC, LEED-CS, LEED for Schools, LEED-CI, and LEED-EB, the minimum program requirements for certification include the following:[3]

- Comply with environmental laws.
- Be a complete, permanent building or space.
- Use a reasonable site boundary.
- Comply with minimum floor area requirements (1,000 square feet minimum, or 250 square feet minimum for LEED-CI).
- Comply with minimum occupancy rates of one or more full-time-equivalent occupant to be eligible for Indoor Environmental Quality optional credits.
- Commit to sharing whole-building energy and use data with the USGBC and/or the Green Building Certification Institute for five years after occupancy, even if ownership or tenancy changes.
- Comply with a minimum gross floor area to gross land ratio of 2 percent.

Additional information on Minimum Program Requirements can be found in the USGBC document "LEED 2009 MPR Supplemental Guidance."

THE PROCESS

The USGBC develops the LEED rating systems, but since 2009, the Green Building Certification Institute (GBCI) has administered the registration and certification of buildings. The GBCI describes the process, which is administered using the LEED Online v3 tool, as follows:

1. Register the project with LEED Online at the GBCI website and pay the registration fee. LEED Online includes an optional ratings system selector questionnaire to help determine which rating system is most appropriate.

2. For LEED-CS, an optional precertification application may be made. The GBCI's formal recognition of the developer's goal for the project to achieve LEED-CS certification may be helpful in marketing to potential tenants.

3. Build the online credit scorecard by selecting the optional credits that will be pursued. All project team members may be granted access; in addition, LEED Online v3 allows the project administrator to assign responsibility for credits to different team members by name.

4. Access credit forms from the project scorecard and document credit compliance online.

5. Upon completing project documentation, submit it for review and certification.

6. Commit to providing whole-building energy and water usage data to the USGBC and/or the GBCI for at least the first five years after occupancy begins. This commitment must be honored even if the owner or tenant changes.

THE COST

The cost for registering a commercial project in 2010 was $900 for USGBC members and $1,200 for nonmembers. Project certification rates in 2010 are listed in Table 10-1.

Additional potential costs include those for implementing some of the prerequisites and optional credits, along with the time spent to document credits, which will vary by project and project team. As with any rating system, there will likely be a learning curve while project team members familiarize themselves with LEED v3 and its requirements. Project teams may include a LEED consultant. The *LEED Reference Guide for Green Building Design and Construction* covers LEED-NC, LEED-CS, and LEED for Schools and is available from the USGBC for $115 to $180 depending on membership status, whether purchased with a training workshop, and whether in an e-book or hard-copy format.

THIRD-PARTY VERIFICATION

Before 2009, the USGBC provided third-party verification for LEED certification with assistance from independently contracted reviewers. The GBCI now administers LEED building certification, working with 10 or more certification bodies. These national and international firms are accredited to certify services and products to International Organization for Standardization (ISO) standards.[5] The GBCI conducts independent quality assurance audits of certification reviews.

TABLE 10-1 PROJECT CERTIFICATION RATES

	Less than 50,000 Square Feet	50,000–500,000 Square Feet	More Than 500,000 Square Feet	Appeals (if applicable)
LEED 2009; New Construction, Commercial Interiors, Schools, Core and Shell Full Certification	Fixed rate	Based on square footage	Fixed rate	Per credit
Design Review				
USGBC Members	$2,000	$0.04/sf	$20,000	$500
Nonmembers	$2,250	$0.045/sf	$22,500	$500
Expedited Fee*	$5,000 regardless of square footage			$500
Construction Review				
USGBC Members	$500	$0.010/sf	$5,000	$500
Nonmembers	$750	$0.015/sf	$7,500	$500
Expedited Fee*	$5,000 regardless of square footage			$500
Combined Design and Construction Review				
USGBC Members	$2,250	$0.045/sf	$22,500	$500
Nonmembers	$2,750	$0.055/sf	$27,500	$500
Expedited Fee*	$10,000 regardless of square footage			$500
LEED for Existing Buildings	Fixed rate	Based on square footage	Fixed rate	Per credit
Initial Certification Review				
USGBC Members	$1,500	$0.03/sf	$15,000	$500
Nonmembers	$2,000	$0.04/sf	$20,000	$500
Expedited Fee*	$10,000 regardless of square footage			$500
Recertification Review**				
USGBC Members	$750	$0.015/sf	,$7,500	$500
Nonmembers	$1,000	$0.02/sf	$10,000	$500
Expedited Fee*	$10,000 regardless of square footage			$500
Credit Interpretation Rulings (for all Rating Systems)				$220

* In addition to regular review fee.

** The Existing Building Recertification Review fee is due when the customer submits the application for recertification review.

Source: © 2008 Green Building Certification Institute. All Rights Reserved.[4]

The GBCI was created in 2008 with the support of the USGBC as a separate nonprofit entity to administer LEED professional credentialing in compliance with the American National Standards Institute (ANSI).

CERTIFICATION CRITERIA

Project checklists of available optional credits and mandatory prerequisites, along with rating system documents for LEED-NC, LEED-CS, LEED for Schools, and the other LEED 2009 rating systems, are available for free download from the USGBC website. The 100-plus page rating systems documents describe the credits and prerequisites, including intent and potential technologies and strategies. It is a very useful document to refer to when considering whether to pursue certification. The more extensive *LEED Reference Guide for Green Building Design and Construction* describes issues to consider, related credits, implementation options, documentation guidance, and other resources. The *Reference Guide* is available for purchase from the USGBC.

The following overviews of the LEED-NC, LEED-CS and LEED for Schools rating systems are summarized from the *LEED Reference Guide.*

Sustainable Sites

This category addresses the selection and design of the site for development. Up to 26 points are available for LEED-NC, 28 for LEED-CS, and 24 for Schools. Credits are awarded for measures such as selecting sites that minimize the environmental impact of development, facilitating alternative transportation, designing sustainable landscaping, reducing heat island effects, and managing surface water.

Sustainable Sites Prerequisites

■ *Construction Activity Pollution Prevention:* For LEED-NC, LEED-CS, and LEED for Schools, create and implement an erosion and sediment control plan in conformance with the referenced standards.

■ *Environmental Site Assessment:* Required for LEED for Schools only. Perform an environmental site assessment to determine if the site is contaminated. Sites previously used as landfill are not eligible to participate in LEED for Schools.

Figure 10-2 This rain garden uses native perennial plants, a drain tile system, and a water-level control system to manage stormwater. Located on the University of Minnesota Duluth campus, this rain garden can hold up to 60,000 gallons of water. *Photo courtesy of Karen Jeannette.*

Water Efficiency

This category focuses on reducing indoor and outdoor water use. Up to 10 points are available for LEED-NC and LEED-CS, and 11 points for LEED for Schools.

Water Efficiency Prerequisite

■ *Water use reduction:* For LEED-NC, LEED-CS, and LEED for Schools, reduce water use (exclusive of irrigation) by 20 percent in aggregate over water use baseline, calculated according to the information in the *Reference Manual.*

Energy and Atmosphere

This category concentrates on reducing energy consumption. There are up to 35 points available for LEED-NC, 37 points for LEED-CS, and 33 points for LEED for Schools. Credits include optimizing energy performance, implementing on-site renewable energy, and planning measurement and verification of building energy consumption. There are three prerequisites in this category, all of which apply to LEED-NC, LEED-CS, and LEED for Schools.

Figure 10-3 This mixed-use development under construction on a former parking lot in downtown New Haven, Connecticut, addresses many Sustainable Sites credits. Developed and designed by Becker + Becker of Fairfield, Connecticut, this 700,000-square-foot project is in the LEED for Neighborhood Development pilot program.

Energy and Atmosphere Prerequisites

- *Fundamental Commissioning of Building Energy Systems:* Perform commissioning process activities for heating, ventilating, air conditioning and refrigeration systems (HVAC&R), domestic hot water systems, renewable energy systems, and daylighting and lighting controls.

- *Minimum Energy Performance:* There are two options for meeting this requirement:

  - *Whole-Building Energy Simulation:* Demonstrate an improvement in the proposed building performance rating of 10 percent for new construction or 5 percent for major renovations over the baseline building performance in ASHRAE 90.2-2007.

  - *Prescriptive Compliance Path:* Comply with the prescriptive requirements of ASHRAE Advanced Energy Design Guide, Advanced Energy Design Guide for K-12 School Buildings, or Advanced Buildings™ Core Performance™ Guide, as applicable.

- *Fundamental Refrigerant Management:* New HVAC&R equipment shall use no chlorofluorocarbon-based refrigerants. If reusing existing equipment, complete a CFC phase-out plan.

Materials and Resources

This category focuses on resource efficiency, including reusing an existing building; reusing materials and using materials that have recycled content, are rapidly renewable, and are regionally available; and reducing construction waste. Up to 14 points are available in LEED-NC; 13 for LEED-CS and LEED for Schools.

Materials and Resources Prerequisite

- For LEED-NC, LEED-CS, and LEED for Schools, provide a dedicated area for collecting and storing recycling.

Indoor Environmental Quality

This category is concerned with items such as indoor air quality, occupant comfort, and daylight. There are up to 15 points available for LEED-NC, 12 for LEED-CS, and 19 for LEED for Schools. Credits are available for using low-emitting materials; providing lighting controls, daylight, and views; and ensuring thermal comfort.

If the project does not serve at least one annualized full-time-equivalent occupant, it is not eligible to receive the optional credits in this category.[6] The prerequisites are mandatory, regardless of occupant numbers.

Indoor Environmental Prerequisites

■ *Minimum Indoor Air Quality Performance:* For LEED-NC, LEED-CS, and LEED for Schools, the mechanical or natural ventilation system must comply with the referenced part of ASHRAE Standard 62.1-2007.

■ *Environmental Tobacco Smoke Control:* For LEED-NC and LEED-CS, prohibit smoking in the building or provide smoking rooms designed to contain and remove smoke. For LEED for Schools, prohibit smoking in the building. For all, comply with requirements regarding smoking outdoors.

■ *Minimum Acoustical Performance:* Required for NC-Schools only. Meet acoustical requirements for sound-absorptive finishes and HVAC background noise for classrooms and other core learning spaces.

Innovation in Design

Points may be awarded in this category for exceeding the requirements or for performance innovations not addressed in LEED. A point is available for having a LEED Accredited Professional on the project team, and for LEED for Schools for integrating the high-performance building features into the curriculum. Up to six points are available. There are no prerequisites in this category.

Regional Priority

This category does not offer new credits but rather offers bonus points as incentives to address regional priorities. The regional priorities are determined at registration by the project's zip code, and can also be found on the USGBC website. Up to four points can be achieved. There are no prerequisites in this category.

Figure 10-4 In this firehouse, 87 percent of regularly occupied spaces have natural daylight, and 97 percent of those have views to the outdoors. *Photo courtesy of Michael Urbanek Photography.*

Climate: Hot-Dry (Zone 3)

Size: 12,400 square feet, two stories

Construction Cost: $4,785,619

Completion Date: 2008

Owner: City of San Jose

Architect: RRM Design Group, San Luis Obispo, California

Mechanical/Plumbing Engineer: Brummel, Myrick and Associates, San Luis Obispo, California

Electrical Engineer: Thoma Electric, San Luis Obispo, California

Structural Engineer: Biggs Cardosa, Inc., San Francisco, California

Cost Estimator: NJF Consulting, Sausalito, California

Constructor: Farotte Construction, Gilroy, California

Points Achieved: 34, Silver (LEED-NC v2.2)

San Jose Fire Station No. 35 34 Points Achieved (Silver Certification)	
Sustainable Sites	8
Water Efficiency	3
Energy & Atmosphere	2
Materials & Resources	7
Indoor Environmental Quality	11
Innovation & Design	3

This firehouse is built on a 0.9-acre urban site on a former parking lot. It includes an administrative suite, an apparatus bay and support spaces, and fire-fighter house. The City of San Jose requires that buildings be at least LEED certified, which presented some challenges for this building type. For example, designing for efficient firefighter operations and quick response times governed building orientation. With parts of the firehouse operating round-the-clock daily and requiring constant climate control, meeting the requirements of Energy & Atmosphere Prerequisite 2 was only possible with an accompanying in-depth narrative explaining the unique demands of a firehouse.

Additional Costs

Additional costs for pursuing LEED certification included $40,000 in documentation fees, $450 in registration fees, $1,750 in certification fees ($1,250 for the design review and $500 for the construction review), and $46,600 in commissioning fees.[7]

Sustainable Features

The firehouse is built on a previously developed site; the stormwater control system eliminates the majority of toxic solids before returning it to the city system; and native drought-tolerant landscaping was used to reduce irrigation. Water use is 45 percent less than conventional buildings, owing to dual-flush toilets, low-flow showers and kitchen sinks, and ultra-low-flow lavatories. The building exceeds the requirements of California's energy code Title 24 by 16 percent. The building's materials contain 23 percent recycled content, and 21 percent of products in the building were manufactured or harvested from within 500 miles of the project site. Low-emitting adhesives and sealants, paints and coats, flooring systems, composite wood, and agrifiber products were used. Eighty-seven percent of regularly occupied spaces have natural daylight, and 97 percent of those had views to the outdoors. More than 75 percent of construction waste was diverted from the landfill.[8]

Figure 10-5 The landscaping vegetation is native and drought-resistant. *Photo courtesy of Michael Urbanek Photography.*

Tips from the Architect

Job Captain Jennifer Brennan, LEED AP, and Principal Stacey White, AIA, LEED AP, offered the following advice for design teams pursuing LEED certification:

■ "Assemble your entire project team and start to incorporate LEED into the project at the earliest point in the project possible.

■ "Perform a thorough LEED charrette during the schematic design phase with the entire design team to establish a strategy and documentation responsibilities, and establish the project standards to include coordinated full-time-equivalent building occupants, list of regularly occupied spaces, common room square footages, etc.

■ "Incorporate LEED documentation and threshold requirements into both the specifications and construction drawings, as applicable.

■ "The LEED project administrator must take an active role in maintaining and coordinating the documentation in both the design and construction phases."[9]

Brennan and White see the strengths and weaknesses of LEED as follows:

STRENGTHS

■ "The LEED program holds the entire project team, including owners, designers, and builders, accountable to achieving set thresholds and following through with their intent of pursuing sustainable features in their building projects. Often, difficulties during the implementation stage of the project create temptations to compromise on quality, efficiency, and durability. By establishing LEED as a goal, it provides the team the necessary framework to keep those qualities as priorities."[10]

WEAKNESSES

■ "With such specific measures addressed by each point, clients can tend to pursue only those sustainable features that may earn them LEED points, and tend to stop thinking innovatively.

■ "We also found that there was no way for our project team to hold the USGBC reviewers to their own deadlines, which has the potential to strain the relationship with the client when the project team cannot deliver LEED updates as scheduled."[11]

Tips from the Builder

Gary Farotte, owner of Farotte Construction, has worked on two LEED-certified projects for the city of San Jose, including Firehouse No. 35. He suggests, "Get involved in the process early on, even in the bidding stages." He says of LEED, "It's leading the industry to a green process. It's causing us to reanalyze the entire construction process." He sees this as the strength of LEED, but notes, "The industry is not mature enough to do this without extra cost."[12]

University of
Minnesota–Duluth
Labovitz School of
Business and Econom-
ics, Duluth, Minnesota

Figure 10-6 People spend much time indoors during the academic year due to the cold climate, so the building was designed with direct outdoor views from most offices for full-time employees. *Photo by James Steinkamp. © 2009 Steinkamp Photography.*

Climate: Very Cold (Zone 7)

Size: 66,909 square feet; three stories plus partial basement

Construction Cost: $17.9 million

Completion Date: 2008

Owner: Board of Regents, University of Minnesota

Architect of Record: Perkins+Will, Chicago, Illinois, and Minneapolis, Minnesota

Associate Architect: SJA Architects, Duluth, Minnesota

MEP-FP-Tech Engineers: Gausman & Moore, Duluth and St. Paul, Minnesota

Structural Engineer: Meyer Borgman Johnson, Duluth, Minnesota

Civil Engineer: Short Elliott Hendrickson, Inc., Duluth, Minnesota

Landscape Architect: oslund.and.associates, Chicago, Illinois

General Contractor: Oscar J. Boldt Construction, Cloquet, Minnesota

Points Achieved: 42, Gold (LEED-NC v.2.1)

Labovitz School of Business and Economics, Duluth, Minnesota Points Achieved (Gold Certification)	
Sustainable Sites	6
Water Efficiency	3
Energy & Atmosphere	9
Materials & Resources	7
Indoor Environmental Quality	12
Innovation & Design	5

The building is located on an urban campus on a three-acre site. It consists of a 150-seat auditorium, a two-story classroom wing, and a two-story administrative block, all organized around a three-story skylit common area. In addition to being LEED certified, the building also met the requirements of the Benchmarks and Beyond (B3)—Minnesota Sustainable Building Guidelines, as required for state-funded buildings.

Sustainable Features

The cold climate made energy efficiency and occupant well-being priorities for the client. Occupants spend much time indoors during the academic year, so the building was designed with direct outdoor views for the vast majority of offices for full-time employees. Natural daylight was also considered in the layout of classroom and student common areas. Occupancy and daylighting sensors in all occupied areas result in an energy-efficient lighting system.

Figure 10-7 Energy models were created at three different points in the design process. The project achieved eight LEED points by being 51 percent more energy efficient than ASHRAE 90.1-1999. *Photo by James Steinkamp. © 2009, Steinkamp Photography.*

Figure 10-8 The 150-seat auditorium, two-story classroom wing, and two-story administrative block are organized around a three-story skylit common area. *Photo by James Steinkamp.* © *2009, Steinkamp Photography.*

The project pursued LEED's Whole Building Energy Simulation and achieved eight points by being 51 percent more energy efficient than ASHRAE 90.1-1999. Minnesota's B3 program required energy models at three different points in the design process, to analyze the building envelope, mechanical system, and lighting scheme. By creating multiple energy models, designers were able to respond and modify the design to create a more energy-efficient building. "A current weakness of the LEED certification program is that it only requires an energy model to be done at the completion of design," says Mark Walsh, AIA, LEED AP, associate principal at Perkins + Will. "Energy savings have been given a greater weighting in LEED 2009; but in order to be truly effective, the energy modeling process needs to be incorporated into the building design process."[13]

Additional Costs

Meeting the requirements of the B3 program resulted in additional services for design fees of $150,000, which Perkins + Will estimates would have been halved if only LEED had been pursued. The owner is estimated to have incurred an additional $20,000 for an energy modeling consultant. There were also $2,162.50 of LEED design review and appeal fees.[14]

Tips from the Architect

Walsh said, "It is extremely important to engage the entire design team—engineers, landscape architect, designers, energy modelers, client, and others—early in the design of the building in order for a project to be successful and sustainable. Determining responsibility and procedure for implementation and documentation is crucial in accomplishing a complete LEED submittal in a timely manner."[15]

Tips from the Builder

Brian Durand, senior project manager for Oscar J. Boldt Construction, advises, "Be prepared. Understand up front which credits are being pursued, which are achievable, and if any additional credits are reasonably achievable. It's very important that the products and materials are clearly specified with regard to recycled content, rapidly renewable, certified wood, etc. for credits intending to be pursued." Regarding additional costs for pursuing certification, Durand says, "There may be some additional time and money spent on the first LEED project a firm does; however, once familiar with the process and what works well, there does not seem to be a significant additional cost."

Durand found LEED Online to be user-friendly. "LEED is an accurate way to measure the sustainability of each type of project (new construction, remodel, residential, etc.)." He cautioned, however, "If not prepared, and without an understanding of what is being pursued and how it is tracked and documented, it can be very time-consuming."[16]

Figure 10-9 The campus expansion included the Kasych Family Pavilion (right), a new inpatient tower of approximately 270,000 square feet. *Photo © 2008, Matt Wargo Photography.*

Climate: Cold (Zone 5)

Size: This expansion project included these LEED certified elements: a new 130,000-square-foot medical office building; a 5-level parking garage; and a new inpatient tower of approximately 270,000 square feet, the Kasych Family Pavilion. The expansion also included: renovation of approximately 100,000 square feet of existing hospital space; two 2-level parking decks, with approximately 900 spaces for public parking; and a pedestrian bridge connecting the new medical office building to existing facilities.

Construction Cost: $134 million

Completion Date: 2008

Owner: Lehigh Valley Health Network, Allentown, Pennsylvania

Architect of Record and Medical Planning: FreemanWhite, Inc., Charlotte, North Carolina

Building Design Consultant: Venturi Scott Brown & Associates, Philadelphia, Pennsylvania

Civil Engineer: The Pidcock Company, Allentown, Pennsylvania

Mechanical/Electrical/Plumbing Engineer and LEED Services: TLC Engineering for Architecture, Nashville, Tennessee

Structural Engineer: O'Donnell & Naccarato, Inc., Bethlehem, Pennsylvania

Construction Manager/Contractor: The Whiting-Turner Contracting Company, Allentown, Pennsylvania

Points Achieved: 30 points, Certified (LEED-NC v2.2)

Lehigh Valley Health Network—Cedar Crest Expansion Allentown, Pennsylvania 30 Points Achieved (Certified Level)	
Sustainable Sites	4
Water Efficiency	2
Energy & Atmosphere	3
Materials & Resources	5
Indoor Environmental Quality	12
Innovation & Design	4

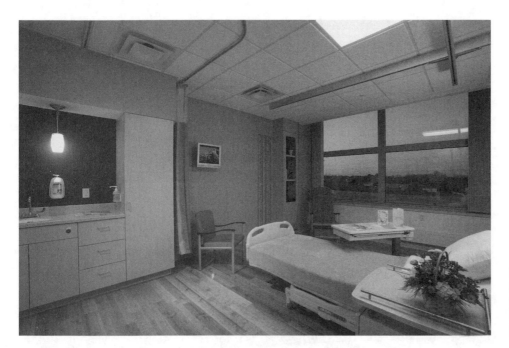

Figure 10-10 All patient rooms have a ceiling lift to prevent injuries to staff and patients. This room is in the Transitional Open Heart Unit. *Photo © 2008, Matt Wargo Photography.*

This expansion and renovation accommodated additional inpatient beds, surgery, emergency department capacity, and support service space. The expansion was designed in response to a larger and aging population in the service area. Inpatient areas include private patient rooms with overnight areas for family members.

Sustainable Features

The design of the Kasych Family Pavilion incorporates recycled building materials, maximizes natural light, uses motion sensors to control lights, and employs energy-efficient mechanical equipment. Many construction materials came from within a 500-mile radius of the site. "Complying with LEED requirements can provide opportunities and unique challenges in a hospital facility," said Chris Richardson, AIA, MBA, managing principal of FreemanWhite. "Clinical function and operational effectiveness do not always parallel the requirements and objectives in LEED certification. For example, the team investigated the use of sensor-controlled water faucets in clinical environments and found that in some instances they wouldn't meet the needs required by the clinical function. Additionally, certain areas of the hospital require privacy and security, which eliminated the ability to provide windows, and thus could not count as part of the areas contributing to daylighting or views required to satisfy the LEED daylighting point criteria. Through dialogue and collaboration the design team reviewed the clinical integrity of these issues, as well as the LEED objectives to define an appropriate strategy for achieving LEED certification. Specifically, sensor faucets were not included, and daylighting

and views were enhanced in other areas of the hospital in an effort to comply with the LEED requirements."[17]

Additional Costs

The team engaged an outside consultant to coordinate LEED certification efforts for a fee of approximately $100,000.[18]

Tips from the Architect

Chris Richardson, AIA, of FreemanWhite says of pursuing LEED certification, "The process challenges the design and construction team to examine how they design and construct facilities, and look for opportunities to improve the effect the facility has during its construction and its effect on occupants after construction. Many of the initiatives can be accomplished with little or no cost. Some provide a payback within a reasonable time."[19]

Figure 10-11 This education center, awash in natural daylight, is used for community education events and employee training. A conference room opens off of it. *Photo © 2008, Matt Wargo Photography.*

RESOURCES

Green Building Certification Institute, www.gbci.org: Additional information on project certification, LEED Online v3, and professional credentials can be found at this website.

LEEDUser, www.LEEDUser.com: BuildingGreen, in collaboration with YRG Sustainability and other LEED experts, has developed the LEEDUser online tool available by subscription. The tool provides tips, documentation and credit guidance, and best practices and resources.

Real Life LEED®, www.reallifeleed.com: This blog by Joel McKellar contains tips about taking the LEED exam for professional accreditation, information on different credits, links to other resources, and opinions and commentary.

U.S. Green Building Council, www.usgbc.org: The LEED 2009 rating systems and checklists are available for free download from this website. Reference guides that provide more information about credit and documentation requirements and resources are available for purchase. The site also offers information on green building (including links to research publications, links to other websites, and LEED project case studies); USGBC educational programs; and LEED reference documents, templates, and tools.

NOTES

1. Marie Coleman, Communications Coordinator, USGBC, email to the author, July 8, 2009.

2. *GBCI Policy Manual for LEED Green Building Rating Systems Minimum Program Requirements*, www.gbci.org; accessed July 2, 2009.

3. From "LEED 2009 Minimum Program Requirements," approved April 2009, on www.gbci.org/DisplayPage.aspx?CMSPageID=130; accessed July 30, 2009.

4. www.gbci.org/DisplayPage.aspx?CMSPageID=127; accessed June 26, 2009.

5. "About GBCI" from www.gbci.org, accessed July 3, 2009, and USGBC news release, "Certification Bodies Announced for LEED Green Building Ratings Systems," July 29, 2008.

6. *GBCI Policy Manual*, www.gbci.org; accessed July 2, 2009.

7. In an email attachment sent to the author on July 27, 2009 by Brenda Grijalva, Marketing Coordinator, RRM Design Group.

8. Ibid.

9. Ibid.

10. Ibid.

11. Ibid.

12. Gary Farotte, Owner, Farotte Construction, telephone interview with the author, August 3, 2009.

13. Mark Walsh, AIA, LEED AP, Associate Principal, Perkins + Will, Chicago, Illinois, email from Amie Oberstar to the author, June 11, 2009.

14. Additional costs information from Amie M. Oberstar, Marketing Manager, Perkins + Will, Chicago, Illinois, email to the author, June 11, 2009.

15. Mark Walsh, AIA, LEED AP, Associate Principal, Perkins + Will, Chicago, Illinois, in June 11, 2009 email attachment from Amie Oberstar to the author.

16. Brian Durand, Senior Project Manager, Oscar J. Boldt Construction, email to the author, August 5, 2009.

17. In July 10, 2009 email attachment to the author sent by Karen Broome, Director of Marketing, FreemanWhite, Inc.

18. Ibid.

19. Ibid.

11

LOCAL AND REGIONAL COMMERCIAL PROGRAMS

Since the late 1990s, the number of green building programs for municipal and commercial buildings has soared. An American Institute of Architects (AIA) study found that the path followed by communities developing green building programs is similar.[1] Typically, the planning department includes language about sustainable development in a master plan. Next, one of two things tends to occur: either a legislator or executive creates an entity to study existing sustainability policies and make recommendations, which may become policies or ordinances; or the planning department may rewrite zoning regulations to include green design.

Often green building programs begin as requirements for government-funded projects to meet energy-efficiency measures. Requirements for the greening of municipal projects may then spill over into the private sector. In developing standards, local leaders often turn to existing rating systems. For example, LEED® initiatives can be found in 43 states,[2] and Green Globes® is formally recognized in 19 states.[3]

EXAMPLES OF LOCAL AND REGIONAL COMMERCIAL PROGRAMS

Many localities that have green commercial building programs offer voluntary guidelines and incentives, such as expedited permitting, lower permit fees, or awards programs. Others require that construction comply with existing building assessment systems or with criteria that are unique to the locale. Here are examples of some local and regional programs.

Austin Energy Green Building, Austin, Texas

Austin has a long history of promoting green buildings. In 1991, it created a rating tool for single-family homes. In 2000, Austin City Council passed a resolution requiring all municipal buildings over 5,000 square feet to meet the requirements of LEED Silver. In 2005, the Austin Energy Green Building™ (AEGB) rating system for commercial buildings evolved. In addition to offering rating tools for commercial, residential, and multifamily housing, Austin Energy offers the Sustainable Building Sourcebook, workshops, case studies, and other resources.

The AEGB rating tool has eight basic requirements or prerequisites, which include building systems commissioning and construction waste management. A total of 77 points are available in the following categories: Team, Site, Energy, Water, Indoor Environmental Quality, Materials and Resources, Education, and Innovation. Between one and five stars are awarded, depending on the number of points achieved, with one star for meeting the basic requirements and five stars for achieving 59 or more points.

The Chicago Standard

The Chicago Standard, adopted in 2004 for public buildings, is based on LEED-NC v. 2.1 (which had 46 total points) and requires that the 26 credits considered most applicable to Chicago be earned. Achieving alternate credits so that municipal buildings may receive a higher level of LEED certification is encouraged but not required. The Green Permit Program expedites the permitting process for construction projects that employ green strategies.

California Green Building Standards Code

In 2008, the California Building Standards Commission adopted the California Green Standards Code; it will become mandatory beginning in

2010. The goal of the code is to reduce energy use by 15 percent more than 2008 standards, and water use by 20 percent with a 50 percent reduction in landscaping water use. This new "green building code" is the first such statewide measure adopted in the United States. Local regulations are permitted to mandate sustainable measures that exceed the statewide requirements.

This code follows an executive order issued in 2004, directing new state construction to meet LEED Silver certification levels with a minimum 20 percent reduction of energy purchases by 2015 for state-owned buildings. The reduction is as compared to Titles 20 and 24 nonresidential standards adopted in 2003.

Massachusetts Zero Net Energy Building

In 2006, the Commonwealth of Massachusetts' Executive Office for Administration and Finance issued a bulletin requiring that all executive agencies follow new sustainable design and construction standards for new

Figure 11-1 There are 372 solar panels in this photovoltaic system on the roof of the Williams Building in Boston. *Image courtesy of DOE.*

construction and major renovations. The requirements, called Massachusetts LEED Plus, require attaining LEED certification with specific credits that are optional in LEED-NC becoming mandatory under the Massachusetts program. These additional prerequisites included energy performance to exceed the state energy code by at least 20 percent, third-party building commissioning, and meeting Smart Growth criteria.[4]

In 2007, Governor Duval Patrick committed state government to reducing energy use by 20 percent by 2012 and 30 percent by 2030. Then in 2008, the governor established a task force of building and energy industry professionals to advise the state on how to raise green building standards in such a way that private and public buildings, residential and commercial, could reach the goal of being net-zero energy buildings by 2030. Recommendations include establishing energy performance standards for new commercial and home construction and major renovations by 2012.

Collaborative of High Performance Schools (CHPS)

The mission of the Collaborative for High Performance Schools (CHPS) is "to facilitate the design, construction and operation of high performance schools: environments that are not only energy and resource efficient, but also healthy, comfortable, well lit, and containing the amenities for a quality education."[5] The CHPS began in California in 1999; the CHPS criteria for rating California K-12 schools were launched in 2001. Beginning in 2004, the criteria were adapted into programs for Massachusetts, New York, Washington, Texas, Colorado, and the Northeast (Connecticut, Maine, New Hampshire, and Rhode Island). The program applies to new K-12 school construction and major modernizations.

Criteria include acoustics, building commissioning, daylighting, energy efficiency, indoor air quality, preventive maintenance, site protection, sustainable materials, waste reduction, and water conservation. The number of credits and number and type of prerequisites in each category vary regionally based on the climate, state priorities, and practices. Local codes are cited in the criteria to ensure that buildings exceed local requirements, even where local requirements already exceed national ones. Projects meeting the required criteria receiving third-party verification are declared CHPS Verified, while projects using a free self-certification system are certified as CHPS Designed.

Living Building Challenge

The Living Building Challenge is a program of the Cascadia Region Green Building Council, a chapter of the nonprofit U.S. Green Building Council. It is intended for use in any location and building type. It uses as a benchmark what is possible, with the goal of creating self-sustaining buildings that generate their own renewable energy and capture and treat water. There are six performance areas, or "petals": Site, Energy, Materials, Water, Indoor Quality, and Beauty + Inspiration. There are 16 prerequisites within the performance areas; nothing is optional. A petal may be earned by complying with the requirements of that performance area. If requirements for all six areas are met, the building can earn Living Building status. Because the designation is based on actual performance, buildings must be operating for a year before they are evaluated.

Green Building Programs in Our Nation's Communities

In 2007, the AIA contacted 661 cities with populations of 50,000 or more and spoke to representatives of 606 of these cities. They compiled their findings in a report titled, "Local Leaders in Sustainability: A Study of Green Building Programs in Our Nation's Communities." Information collected on commercial programs in these communities is listed in Table 11-1, for which the AIA provided updated information in 2009.

TABLE 11-1 LOCAL AND REGIONAL GREEN BUILDING PROGRAMS FOR MUNICIPAL AND COMMERCIAL CONSTRUCTION

City, State	Year Program Began	Applies to: 1–Municipal 2–Commercial	Website	Notes
Phoenix, Arizona	2005	1		Buildings must only be certifiable. The city has LEED-accredited engineers.
Scottsdale, Arizona	1998	1, 2	www.scottsdaleaz.gov/greenbuilding	The city requires LEED Gold for municipal buildings and periodically updates its checklists to stay current with technology.
Tucson, Arizona	2005	1	In development	There is another landscape ordinance that addresses commercial buildings as well. There are several water-specific regulations. They also have an Office of Conservation AND Sustainable Development.
Alameda, California		1		$100K+ projects must be LEED Gold. Continuation uncertain owing to economic crisis.
Anaheim, California	2007	1, 2	www.anaheim.net (Department of Public Utilities/Green Connection)	
Berkeley, California	2004	1, 2	www.cityofberkeley.info/sustainable	The city is also looking into pushing their energy requirements beyond Title 24.
Burbank, California	2003	2	www.burbankca.org/building/bgreen.htm	It started as a voluntary program. The ratings are 3-tiered and focus more on getting developers to participate rather than worry about the level that is actually attained.
Carlsbad, California	2007	1		New program with plans to continue developing.

(continued)

TABLE 11-1 (*Continued*)

City, State	Year Program Began	Applies to: 1–Municipal 2–Commercial	Website	Notes
Corona, California	2007	1, 2		Voluntary program. Commercial building to 20 pts of LEED checklist. City provides expedited permitting for green projects.
Costa Mesa, California	2007	1, 2	www.ci.costa-mesa.ca.us/ departments/green-building/ green-bldg.htm	LEED standard is used. Mandatory for municipal buildings; voluntary for commercial.
Davis, California		1, 2	www.cityofdavis.org/cdd/ green_building.cfm	LEED is standard for municipal and commercial. No certification requirement, but most new construction projects are going forward with certification.
Fremont, California	2006	1	www.fremont.gov/ Environment/GreenBuilding/ default.htm	Applies to municipal buildings over 10,000 sq. ft. Alameda County also offers free consulting to developers shooting for certification.
Fresno, California	2007	1, 2	www.fresnogreen.net	Build It Green and LEED are used. Plan is tied to planning mostly. Incentives-based program that is tied directly to furthering the community's mandatory green codes.
Glendale, California	2007	2	www.ci.glendale.ca.us	LEED Silver, Gold, and Platinum buildings can earn density bonuses.
Irvine, California	2006	1, 2		Irvine has its own 100 pt. rating system for commercial and residential recognition.
La Mesa, California	2007	1		
Livermore, California	2006	1, 2	In development	The mandatory program will require 20 LEED points for commercial and 50 Build It Green Points for residential.
Long Beach, California	2006	1	www.longbeach.gov/plan/ pb/apd/green/default.asp	The city is also looking into options for a policy regarding private development.
Los Angeles, California	2002	1	eng.lacity.org/projects/sdip/ about_us.htm	The city has a sustainability task force.
Mission Viejo, California	2006	2	cityofmissionviejo.org/depts/ cd/green_building	The program is still in its pilot phase until 2008.
Oakland, California	2005	1, 2	www.sustainableoakland.com	Voluntary for commercial projects. The city has had a Sustainable Community Development initiative since 1998.
Palo Alto, California	2007	1		The city plans on growing the program is exploring mandatory points as an option
Pasadena, California	2006	1, 2	www.ci.pasadena.ca.us/ permitcenter/greencity/ building/gbprogram.asp	Public buildings, 25,000+ sq. ft. commercial, and 4+ story residential projects are required to be LEED certified. It is optional for other development.
Petaluma, California	2006	2	www.cityofpetaluma.net/cdd/ big/index.html	The program is optional for all, and there is a $500 per unit rebate incentive.
Pleasanton, California	2002	1, 2	www.ci.pleasanton.ca.us/ business/planning	The mandatory portions of the program were passed in 2006; before this it only applied to municipal buildings.

(continued)

TABLE 11-1 (*Continued*)

City, State	Year Program Began	Applies to: 1–Municipal 2–Commercial	Website	Notes
Richmond, California	2007	1		LEED Silver is required of municipal buildings. Any project receiving $300,000+ from the city must also earn Silver or 50 Build It Green points.
Sacramento, California	2004	1	www.cityofsacramento.org/ generalservices/sustain/ greengoals.html	The city is also working on reducing fees for private solar generation.
San Buenaventura (Ventura), California	2006	1	www.ci.ventura.ca.us/ GreenVentura	Municipal buildings must be certifiable. The rest is voluntary using LEED and the California Green Builder standards. Voluntary projects are eligible for expedited permitting.
San Diego, California	2002	1, 2	www.sandiego.gov/ environmental-services/ sustainable/index.shtml	San Diego's program comprises a number of ordinances requiring municipal buildings be LEED Silver and providing expedited planning incentives to commercial and multifamily developments.
San Francisco, California	1999	1, 2	www.sfenvironment.org/our_ programs/overview.html?ssi = 8	The city is continuing to advance. This summer the Green Task Force recommended a number of changes, including mandatory standards.
San Jose, California	2001	1	www.sanjoseca.gov/esd/ natural-energy-resources/ greenbuilding.htm	The planning department promotes private green design, but the municipal policy is the only one that is official.
San Leandro, California	2006			San Leandro builders also receive incentives from Alameda County.
San Rafael, California	2007	1, 2	In development	New mandatory program.
Santa Barbara, California	2006	1, 2	www.builtgreensb.org	The policies are voluntary for private development, and permits can be fast-tracked. There is also a solar recognition program to promote the use of solar energy.
Santa Clarita, California	2005	1		The city has a sustainable purchasing guide that covers almost all of the supplies the city buys.
Santa Cruz, California	2006	1, 2	www.ci.santa-cruz.ca.us/pl/ building/green.html	Mandatory minimums combined with incentives.
Santa Monica, California	2000	1	greenbuildings.santa-monica.org	
Santa Rosa, California	2004	1		The city is considering updates to the program to strengthen it and expand its scope.
Sunnyvale, California	2004	1, 2	sunnyvale.ca.gov/Departments/ Community+Development/ Planning+Division/Planning-Green+Buildings.htm	City buildings over 10,000 sq. ft. are covered. The city offers a 5% floor area bonus to commercial developers.
Aurora, Colorado		1		City buildings and buildings receiving city funding must meet LEED Gold.

(continued)

TABLE 11-1 (*Continued*)

City, State	Year Program Began	Applies to: 1—Municipal 2—Commercial	Website	Notes
Boulder, Colorado	1993	1		The residential Green Points system they use is currently being updated again and will likely include commercial and multifamily housing.
Denver, Colorado	2005	1	www.greenprintdenver.org	Currently, the program is a resolution, but that is being strengthened this fall.
Fort Collins, Colorado	1998	1, 2	www.fcgov.com/opserv/pdf/green-bldg.pdf	It is a very flexible program, with different departments having different incentives. The city is currently working to tie everything together.
Stamford, Connecticut	2006	1	In development	The Sustainable Stamford program encourages private sustainable development.
Washington, District of Columbia	2007	1, 2		Large commercial buildings will be required to achieve at least a LEED Certified rating.
Coral Springs, Florida	1, 2			Require submission of LEED checklist to gauge what green aspects are being voluntarily incorporated. Incentives planned.
Gainesville, Florida	2002	1, 2	www.usgbc.org/ShowFile.aspx?DocumentID=1979	Florida cities must be careful in developing Green Building programs due to building concerns regarding hurricanes. The city is working with the state to further coordinate their policy.
Lauderhill, Florida	2006	1, 2		Compliance is voluntary, but all applicable buildings must submit a statement identifying any green design components.
North Miami, Florida		1, 2	www.greennorthmiami.com	LEED Silver required for municipal buildings; voluntary for commercial. Incentives are in place.
St. Petersburg, Florida	2006	2	www.stpete.org/development/developmentreview.htm	Sarasota County is very active in promoting green building. The city program is very informal but there is a very good relationship between developers, planners, and normal citizens.
West Palm Beach, Florida		2		Voluntary standards that incorporate some LEED requirements.
Athens-Clarke County (balance), Georgia	2005	1	www.accplanning.com	In addition to the municipal policy, the city has conservation subdivisions to develop better planned neighborhoods.
Atlanta, Georgia	2003	1	www.atlantaga.gov/client_resources/mayorsoffice/green%20initiative/green%20initiatives.pdf	The EarthCraft Homes program has also been in existence since 1999. Currently, the city is working to shed its reputation for sprawl by developing sustainable communities in addition to single buildings.
Honolulu CDP, Hawaii	2004	1, 2		Commercial, industrial, and hotel development can get a one-year exemption on real property taxes.
Aurora, Illinois		1, 2		Voluntary program using LEED. Mandatory regulations for all municipal structures not far off. Incentives include review time frames and density and lot coverage.

(continued)

TABLE 11-1 (*Continued*)

City, State	Year Program Began	Applies to: 1—Municipal 2—Commercial	Website	Notes
Chicago, Illinois	2004	1	www.cityofchicago.org City Departments, Department of Environment	The success of separate programs is unique to the political culture of the city and the mayor.
Bloomington, Indiana	2007	1, 2	www.bloomington.in.gov/ planning	The city offers bonus density to qualified projects and also has a Green Acres neighborhood program.
Baltimore, Maryland	2008	1, 2	www.baltimorecity.gov/ sustainability	All new construction over a certain sq ft must be LEED "or comparable."
Bowie, Maryland	2003	1	www.cityofbowie.org/green/ green.htm	The program is intentionally vague and does not specify LEED or another guideline. The goal is to promote flexible implementation and avoid focusing solely on points in the rating system.
Gaithersburg, Maryland	2003	1, 2	www.gaithersburgmd.gov/ poi/default.asp?POI_ID= 793&TOC=107;81;388;585;793;	The LEED checklist must be filled out by all applicable development. Incentives to be certified include reduced permit fees and city rebates for LEED fees.
Rockville, Maryland	2010	1, 2	www.rockvillemd.gov/ environment/built/codes.html	All building over 7,000 sq ft must meet LEED certified level, but certification is not required. Incentives planned.
Boston, Massachusetts	2007	1, 2	www.bostongreenbuilding.org	The program is written into the municipal code as Article 80. The city amended the LEED guidelines to include city-specific points for features the community values.
Medford Massachusetts	2005	1	www.medford.org/Pages/ MedfordMA_Energy/FINAL_ LAP.pdf	The city is also pursuing a wind power project.
Quincy, Massachusetts	2006	1		The city is working on updating older municipal buildings as well as greening new construction. There is a de facto commercial policy but the city didn't want to constrict it with a specific guideline. Developers present their projects and itemize green features, then work with planners to improve.
Grand Rapids, Michigan	2005	1		The city is finding better economic arguments for green building, and the planning department regularly promotes green design with commercial developers, although a formal policy has not been developed.
Bloomington, Minnesota	2005	2	www.ci.bloomington.mn.us/ code/Code19_9.html#b19_29 see Section 19.29 (g) (4) (F)	Section G-4-F in the code offers a floor area bonus for a specific zoning district. The city tried to promote mixed-use development for more walkability.
Minneapolis, Minnesota	2006	1, 2		In addition to LEED, green development must be 35% above minimum state energy standards. Due to heating costs in the winter they are primarily concerned with energy efficiency and offer bonus density as an incentive.
St. Paul, Minnesota	2005	1, 2		The city uses ENERGY STAR guidelines for residential. Large commercial structures must go through the Excel Energy program.
Kansas City, Missouri	2004	1	www.kcmo.org/manager/ OEQ/cpp-progress.pdf	The city recently hired a sustainability manager and is currently working on removing barriers to green features within existing code to streamline the process before they worry about expanding the program.

(continued)

TABLE 11-1 (*Continued*)

City, State	Year Program Began	Applies to: 1–Municipal 2–Commercial	Website	Notes
Springfield, Missouri		1	www.springfieldmo.gov/egov/ planning_development/ index.html	Mandate that all city buildings meet LEED Silver levels.
Lincoln, Nebraska		1	www.lincolngreendesign.org	
Las Vegas, Nevada	2006	1	www.sustainlasvegas.com (Not until the end of August)	Las Vegas has established a green building fund to raise money from utility fees and provide grants to cover LEED costs.
Jersey City, New Jersey	2007	1		This policy is conceived as the first of many. They are looking into greening everything, from roofs to parks to piers. The planning department also has latitude to work with tax abatements to incentivize green buildings.
Trenton, New Jersey	2004	2		Mayor Doug Palmer is the head of the Council of Mayors. Recently, he has become more interested in green buildings, and the city plans to become more of an example for other eastern cities to follow.
Albuquerque, New Mexico	2005	1		The city has a strategic plan to meet the 2030 Challenge with goals for each department. Recently, the city began working with a Vancouver consultant to update and expand the green building program.
New York, New York	2005	1	www.nyc.gov/planyc	PlaNYC is a comprehensive sustainability plan with 10 goals and 170 specific initiatives to help meet them. Much of the plan revolves around renovating existing buildings since about 85% of the buildings in New York in 2030 have already been built.
Asheville, North Carolina	2007	1		This new program was passed as a first step, with serious plans to expand it in the next year.
Raleigh, North Carolina		1	www.raleighnc.gov/portal/ server.pt/gateway/PTARGS_ 0_2_306_210_0_43/ http;/pt03/DIG_Web_Content/ news/public/News-PubAff- Three_City_Personnel_ Now-20090122-15000541.html	City structures over 10,000 sq ft must be LEED Silver. Buildings smaller than 10,000 sq ft do not have to become certified, but must have energy saving measures in place that would allow it to become certified.
Wilmington, North Carolina	2005	2	www.stewardshipdev.com	Currently, the Lower Cape Fear Stewardship Development Award Program is voluntary and only provides a building award as an incentive.
Winston-Salem, North Carolina	2006	2	www.cityofws.org/Home/ Departments/Planning/Legacy/ Articles/LegacyToolkit	Winston-Salem is a Sierra Club Cool City. They are currently focused on mixed-use planning and walkability.
Cincinnati, Ohio	2006	2	www.cincinnati-oh.gov/cdap/ pages/-16936-	Cincinnati provides a property tax abatement for private developers. The city is also working with a developer to construct a 68-acre neighborhood to help gather data on pervious pavement and green roofs, in particular.

(*continued*)

TABLE 11-1 (*Continued*)

City, State	Year Program Began	Applies to: 1–Municipal 2–Commercial	Website	Notes
Cuyahoga Falls, Ohio	2005	2		The city provides a density bonus for green development.
Hamilton, Ohio	2007	2		For LEED projects, the city amended the code to allow a density bonus and reduced landscaping requirements.
Eugene, Oregon	2006	1		There has also been an ongoing pilot project to expedite plan checks and provide consulting to developers. The city now has a few accredited staff members and is considering extending the pilot to more projects.
Portland, Oregon	2000	1	www.portlandonline.com/osd	One of the few cities in the country to require new municipal buildings to be Gold rated.
Philadelphia, Pennsylvania	2007	1	www.phila.gov/green/index.html	The city has maintained a sustainability commission, which has recently recommended more transit-oriented development. The planning department is in the process of updating the zoning code as well.
Nashville-Davidson (balance), Tennessee	2007	1, 2		Municipal buildings over 2000 sq. ft. and $2 million must be LEED Certified. Other projects are offered density bonuses to meet the same standard.
Austin, Texas	1991	1, 2	www.ci.austin.tx.us/citymgr/default.htm	The program has been around so long it is just an accepted part of the building process. Planning and permitting have a lot of flexibility with what to offer developers, depending on the part of the city they will be in.
Dallas, Texas	2003	1		Dallas has a pilot program that has partnered with Habitat for Humanity to develop green low-income housing.
Flower Mound, Texas	2004	2	www.flower-mound.com/env_resources/envresources_greenbuilding.php	The program is purely voluntary and offers recognition to applicable buildings.
Frisco, Texas	2001	1, 2	www.friscotexas.gov/Projects_Programs/Green_Building/?id = 155	Residential construction must meet ENERGY STAR standards. Municipal construction must be LEED Silver; and commercial or multifamily buildings have a Frisco specific standard based on LEED.
Houston, Texas	2004	1, 2	www.houstonpowertopeople.com	The city places an emphasis on cooperation between developers and planners. The Quick Start program is designed to provide consultation, and the Houston Hope program targets low-income housing.
Plano, Texas	2006	1		In addition to the municipal LEED requirements, the city has an interdepartmental group to provide education and consultation for private construction.
Salt Lake City, Utah	2005	1, 2	slcgreen.com/pages/hpb.htm	Municipal buildings must be LEED Silver, and buildings over 10,000 sq. ft. receiving city funds must also be LEED Certified.

(*continued*)

TABLE 11-1 (*Continued*)

City, State	Year Program Began	Applies to: 1—Municipal 2—Commercial	Website	Notes
Arlington CDP, Virginia	2000	1, 2	www.arlingtonva.us/ Departments/Environmental Services/epo/Environmental ServicesEpoGreen Buildings.aspx#ACinc	All site plan projects must submit a LEED Scorecard and employ a LEED accredited professional. Certain projects are required to earn 26 points; failure to do so results in a $.03 per sq. ft. fee that is used for green building education.
Chesapeake, Virginia	2007	1		The program is brand new and the next step will be to train municipal employees and conduct an energy audit of existing buildings.
Bellingham, Washington	2005	1		The King County program has expanded to include Bellingham as well. The city is working on a waterfront project as part of the LEED ND pilot.
Seattle, Washington	2000	1, 2	www.seattle.gov/environment	In addition to the requirements for city development, Seattle has a dizzying array of incentives for all kinds of sustainable features.
Shoreline, Washington	2007	1	www.cityofshoreline.com/ cityhall/departments/planning/ sustainable/index.cfm	Progress within the city has been somewhat hampered by concerns that municipal government may not be the best place for such action. They like to take cues from the state, but recently they have begun to consider incentives as an appropriate action.
Madison, Wisconsin	1999	1	www.cityofmadison.com/ Environment/default.htm	The driving principle behind the sustainable development is to earn payback on the investments within 10 years. There is more focus on partnerships, as opposed to policies. They view education as the best incentive.
Milwaukee, Wisconsin	2007	1		The city recently created an office of sustainability, and there is a lot of momentum to keep the program expanding.

Source: Excerpted from Brooks Rainwater and Martin Cooper, *Local Leaders in Sustainability: A Study of Green Building Programs in Our Nation's Communities* (Washington, DC: American Institute of Architects, 2007). Reprinted by permission.

Visitor Center at Zion National Park, Utah

In addition to the many state and local governments that have developed green building programs, the federal government plays a significant role in generating demand for and promoting research in green building practices.

One example of federal research involvement is the Visitor Center at Zion National Park in Utah, where the National Park Service (NPS) and the Department of Energy's National Renewable Energy Laboratory (NREL) combined forces to create a building that performed over 70 percent better than a comparable code-compliant building at no additional construction cost.[6] This was achieved

Figure 11-2 *Photo by Robb Williamson. Courtesy of DOE/NREL.*

through a rigorous whole-building design process, which included numerous whole-building energy and lighting computer simulations throughout the design process.[7]

As shown in Figure 11-2, the building includes a photovoltaic system on the roof and trombe walls for passive heating. The floor also acts as a thermal mass. Natural daylight is supplemented by energy-efficient lighting. An automated system maintains thermal comfort and lighting levels. Figure 11-3 shows one of two passive down-draft cool towers which allow for evaporative cooling without distribution fans. In designing the building's natural ventilation system, the design team was inspired by the natural cooling in the canyon.[8]

Figure 11-3 *Photo by Robb Williamson. Courtesy of DOE/NREL.*

RESOURCES

Local planning or building departments are good resources for information on local or state green building programs. The state department of the environment and local sustainability offices also may be useful. Other resources are as follows.

American Institute of Architects, www.aia.org: The AIA has issued a series of reports with the main title "Local Leaders in Sustainability." The reports cover topics such as green building programs, green counties, green incentives, and green schools.

Database of State Incentives for Renewables & Efficiency, www.dsireusa.org: Lists state, local, utility, and federal incentives for renewable energy and energy-efficient measures.

National Association of Counties, www.naco.org: Maintains a searchable online database of county green programs, policies, and other data.

U.S. Department of Energy High Performance Building Database, eere.buildinggreen.com: Search by building type and size, location, owner name, or project name. Building information categories are: Overview; Process; Finance; Land Use; Site & Water; Energy; Materials; Indoor Environment; Images; Ratings & Awards; Lessons; and Learn More. New projects may also be submitted for inclusion.

U.S. Environmental Protection Agency Clean Energy Clean Energy-Environment State and Local Programs, www.epa.gov/cleanenergy/ energy-programs: Provides tools and technical assistance to state and local governments in their clean energy efforts.

U.S. Green Building Council Links page, www.usgbc.org: Provides links to different government initiatives (at all levels of government) related to green buildings.

NOTES

1. Brooks Rainwater, with Cooper Martin, "Local Leaders in Sustainability: A Study of Green Building Programs in Our Nation's Communities" (Washington, DC: American Institute of Architects, 2007), p. 10.

2. www.usgbc.org/government, "LEED Initiatives in Government and Schools," updated July 1, 2009.

3. GBI press release, "Oregon Office Building Earns Highest Green Globes Rating for Green Design and Sustainable Operations of an Existing Building," July 2, 2009.

4. Thomas Trimarco, Secretary, Executive Office for Administration and Finance, "A & F Bulletin 12- Establishment of Minimum Standards for Sustainable Design and Construction of New Buildings and Major Renovations by Executive Agencies," August 11, 2006, pp. 1–3.

5. www.chps.net; accessed February 20, 2009.

6. Paul A. Torcellini, Ron Judkoff, and Shiela Hayter, NREL, conference paper, "Zion National Park Visitor Center: Significant Energy Savings Achieved through a Whole-Building Design Process," NREL/CP-550-32157, July 2002, p. 1.

7. Ibid.

8. Ibid.

12

INTERNATIONAL RATING SYSTEMS

S ince 1990, when the United Kingdom established the first environmental building assessment system, many other countries have adapted or created their own rating systems specific to their climates and cultural values. In other cases, a project may be certified by a rating system designed for use in another country, such as BREEAM® or LEED®, because the parent company is familiar with that rating system, perceives market cache with that rating system, or for another reason. There are 161 LEED-certified projects outside the United States, in 91 countries.[1] A sampling of rating systems used around the world, including BREEAM, is given in this chapter. Information on LEED can be found earlier in this book.

EXAMPLES OF INTERNATIONAL RATING SYSTEMS

BREEAM

BREEAM, the BRE Environmental Assessment Method, was launched in the United Kingdom in 1990; it subsequently influenced the development of other rating systems, including LEED, Green Globes, and Green Star. More than 100,000 buildings have been certified, making BREEAM the most widely used rating system in the world.

Figure 12-1 These London office towers, designed by Skidmore, Owings & Merrill for British Land, achieved the highest BREEAM rating of Excellent. Combined, the 13-story 201 Bishopsgate and the 35-story Broadgate Tower provide 800,000 square feet of office space and ground-floor bars, cafes, and shopping. At its completion in 2008, 201 Bishopsgate and The Broadgate Tower was the largest speculative office development undertaken in the City of London.

BREEAM has assessment systems for a number of building types, among them Courts, Ecohomes, Industrial, Offices, Healthcare, Prisons, Retail, and Education. It also offers a Bespoke version, which can be tailored to any building type not covered by another system. Credit categories include Management; Health and Wellbeing; Energy; Transport; Water; Materials; Land Use and Ecology; and Pollution. There are four levels of achievement: Pass, Good, Very Good, and Excellent. In order to qualify, buildings must be evaluated by a third-party assessor trained and licensed by the Building Research Establishment (BRE).

BREEAM is administered by the BRE, a subsidiary of the BRE Trust, a charitable company. BRE's operation of BREEAM is accredited under the International Standard for Organization (ISO) 9001.

BREEAM International

More than 3,000 buildings certified by BREEAM have been constructed outside the United Kingdom. In response to demand, in 2008 BRE launched BREEAM Europe and BREEAM Gulf. BREEAM Europe pilot schemes were developed for retail, office, and industrial uses. BREEAM Gulf schemes have been developed for retail, offices, leisure activities, hotels, and apartments.

There is also an International Bespoke BREEAM option, whereby a project team can send project information for BRE to prepare a proposal outlining the fee and time frame for tailoring BREEAM to suit the building type and location. On a country or regional basis, BRE is willing to work with emerging organizations such as Green Building Councils (GBCs) to help standardize the assessment system while accommodating regional variations.

CASBEE

The Comprehensive Assessment System for Building Environmental Efficiency (CASBEE) was developed in Japan. Representatives of the government, academia, and the industry came together in 2001 to create the Japanese GreenBuild Council (JaGBC)/Japan Sustainable Building Consortium (JSBC) and develop CASBEE. The Building Environmental Efficiency (BEE) concept evolved from the World Business Council for Sustainable Development's concept of ecoefficiency.[2]

There are tools in CASBEE for New Construction, Urban Development, Urban Area + Buildings, and Home (Detached House) available in English. Additional programs are in Japanese only, and must be purchased. These include CASBEE for New Construction (brief version—for tailoring by local municipalities), Existing Building, Renovation, and Heat Island. A CASBEE for Predesign is being developed.

About 80 criteria are broken down into four main categories: Energy Efficiency, Resource Efficiency, Local Environment, and Indoor Environment. The BEE assessment further classifies these categories into two other categories, one concerned with the quality of the environment for building users—labeled Q for Quality—and one for the negative environmental impact that might be felt outside the building's enclosure—labeled L for Loading. The Q category includes Indoor Environment, Quality of Service, and Outdoor Environment on Site. The L category includes Energy, Resources, and Materials, and Off-Site Environment. The BEE is determined by dividing the Q-value by the L-value; therefore, the higher the Q-value and lower the L-value, the more sustainable the building. It is possible to rank all buildings by increasing BEE value from class C (poor), class B–, class B+, class A, to class S (excellent).

Green Star

Green Star was developed in Australia in 2003 with the assistance of the BRE and with BREEAM as its basis. Subsequent changes made the assessment methodology more similar to LEED than to BREEAM.[3] In 2009, rating tools were available for Retail, Education, Office Design, Office as Built, and Office Interiors. Pilot programs were underway for industrial, multiunit residential, mixed use, healthcare, and office–existing building.

The categories in which points can be earned are Management, Indoor Environment Quality, Energy; Transport, Water, Materials, Land Use and

Figure 12-2 Two Victoria Avenue in Perth, Australia, achieved the highest Green Star certification of six stars. This 77,500-square-foot office building was designed by Woodhead for Stockland. Sustainable features include operating louvers to reduce heat loads, an active chilled beam system, roof-integrated wind turbines, on-site graywater treatment, and high-performance glazing. *Image courtesy of Stockland.*

Ecology, Emissions, and Innovation. Once a score is established in each category, the categories are weighted by dividing the number of points achieved in a category by the number available, and multiplying by 100 percent. Points that are not achievable in a specific project are excluded from the category total. After an approved third-party assessor reviews the project team's self-assessment score, projects scoring 45 points or more are certified. There are three levels of certification: Four Star Green Certified, signifying "Best Practices" (45 to 59 points required); Five Star Green Certified, signifying "Australian Excellence" (60 to 74 points); and Six Star Green Certified, signifying "World Leadership."

Hong Kong Building Environmental Assessment Method (HK-BEAM)

The Hong Kong Building Environmental Assessment Method (HK-BEAM) applies to new construction and renovations for all building types.

Figure 12-3 Hysan's Hennessy Centre Redevelopment project, designed by Kohn Pederson Fox Associates, is expected to earn Platinum-level certification for both HK-BEAM and LEED upon its completion in 2011. The 36-story, 710,000-square-foot mixed-use office and retail building will incorporate natural daylight and ventilation, low-e double glazing, sunshades designed for different solar orientations, and recycled and recyclable materials. *Image courtesy of Kohn Pederson Fox Associates.*

HK-BEAM assesses the entire building process from planning to construction to management and operation. It is a program of the HK-BEAM Society, a nonprofit organization made up of members from the real estate and building construction professions.

HK-BEAM was developed with BREEAM as a starting point and was first launched in 1996.[4] By early 2009, there were 170 certified buildings, totaling 77 million square feet in Hong Kong and mainland China.[5] The program identifies more than 100 criteria in the following categories: Site Aspects, Material Aspects, Energy Use, Water Use, Indoor Environmental Quality, and Innovations and Additions. Four levels of certification may be achieved, with minimum requirements for both the overall score and the indoor environmental quality (IEQ) score. The levels are Bronze, Above Average (40 percent overall, 45 percent IEQ); Silver, Good (55 percent overall, 50 percent IEQ); Gold, Very Good (65 percent overall, 55 percent IEQ); and Platinum, Excellent (75 percent overall, 65 percent IEQ). Third-party verification by an approved assessor is required.

Estidama's Pearl Rating System

The Pearl Rating System is being developed by Estidama ("Estidama" is Arabic for "sustainability") by the Abu Dhabi Urban Planning Council. Estidama was launched in late 2008 in response to the impact of rapid development in Abu Dhabi. This system is described as an aspiration, "an overarching way of viewing all aspects of our life based on its four pillars, environmental, economic, social, and culture, to ensure that its sustainable goals and aspirations are well rounded."[6] The Pearl Rating System, originally drafted in 2007, was being restructured as this was being written. Estidama intends to have core criteria that apply to all building types, rather than multiple tools. The five categories of criteria are expected to be Living Systems, Livable City, Precious Water, Resourceful Energy, and Stewarding Materials. Estidama also intends to align many of the Pearl Rating System criteria with BREEAM, LEED, and Green Star, with the expectation that project teams may seek dual certification.

SBTool

The SBTool is a framework for a building assessment system for commercial, residential, and mixed-use new and existing construction, and it is intended as a toolkit for a national or regional organization to use to develop a local sustainable building assessment system. Because the SBTool is designed to develop an assessment system specific to a particular region, it requires expertise from the national or regional third-party organization tailoring the tool. SBTool had been used in 20 countries as of mid-2009.

In 1996, a section of Natural Resources Canada, now known as CanmetENERGY, initiated a research project in whole-building assessment; it presented the resulting GBTool at an international conference in Vancouver in 1998. In 2002, it turned over the GBTool to the International Initiative for a Sustainable Built Environment (iiSBE), an international collaborative nonprofit organization, at which time the framework was renamed SBTool.

To implement the system, the iiSBE provides a series of Microsoft Excel spreadsheets for download from its website, www.iisbe.org. Once the third-party organization uses the SBTool to establish scope, eligible occupancy types, and locally relevant benchmarks and weights, individual teams can use the tailored SBTool to assess a specific project. Criteria include site selection, project planning, and development; energy and resource consumption; environmental loadings; indoor environmental quality; service quality; social and economic aspects; and cultural and perceptual aspects. Design teams can use the SBTool to set performance targets and to self-assess a performance score. Teams submit the project's score to an independent assessor for review. The independent assessor forwards the reviewed assessment to the iiSBE for quality assurance and certification.

GULF ISLANDS OPERATIONS CENTER, SIDNEY, BRITISH COLUMBIA

The headquarters building for the Gulf Islands National Park Reserve was assessed using both the SBTool and LEED. Designed by McFarland Marceau Architects Ltd. of Vancouver, British Columbia, for Parks Canada, Public Works and Government Services Canada, the three-story building houses park operations and administrative staff. It has a heavy timber structure and an open atrium design that allows for natural daylighting and ventilation. Other sustainable features include an ocean-based geothermal system, a photovoltaic system that provides 20 percent of the building's energy requirements, rain harvesting, and façades designed in response to their orientation. Using the SBTool, the building received a total weighted building score of 3.3, Good Practice or Better. It was certified under LEED Canada-NC v1.0 as the first LEED Platinum building in Canada.

Gulf Islands Operations Center Relative Performance Results with SBTool 0 = Acceptable Practice, 3 = Good Practice, and 5 = Best Practice		
	Active Weights	Weighted Scores
Site Selection, Project Planning, and Development	11%	3.0
Energy and Resource Consumption	19%	3.9
Environmental Loadings	29%	2.8
Indoor Environmental Quality	14%	4.2
Service Quality	17%	3.0
Social and Economic Aspects	6%	3.3
Cultural and Perceptual Aspects	4%	4.3
Total Weighted Building Score Relative Performance Level: Good Practice or Better		3.3

Gulf Islands Operations Center LEED Canada-NC v1.0		
	Points Achieved	Points Available
Sustainable Sites	10	14
Water Efficiency	5	5
Energy & Atmosphere	16	17
Materials & Resources	7	14
Indoor Environmental Quality	12	15
Innovation & Design	5	5
Total Platinum Certification	55	70

Project Architect Ron Kato, MAIBC, LEED AP, said he found the SBTool "allows too much subjectivity in its responses and weighting, given its objective of being a one-size-fits-all global assessment tool."[7]

Stephen Pope, OAA, FRAIC, sustainable building design specialist for Natural Resources Canada Sustainable Buildings & Communities, has been involved with the SBTool and LEED Canada since 1998. Because of his role in the Gulf Islands review as assessment team leader, iiSBE Canada 2008, we asked for his thoughts on the SBTool and LEED.[8]

INTERVIEW WITH STEPHEN POPE, OAA, FRAIC, ON LEED AND THE SBTOOL

Q: What, if any, advantage in terms of building performance did SBTool have as compared to LEED?

A: SBTool was designed to feature a common number of environmental performance measures where the performance areas could be scored using different point weights responding to local environmental priorities. In this way, meaningful local performance assessments could be developed, in addition to performance that could be compared across national or bioregional borders. The tool was designed at a time when many different countries were developing their own national assessment tools, and an international framework committee was formed to guide the direction of the tool. The assessment areas and mix of measures are therefore selected and vetted by an international expert audience.

A restriction of this developmental foundation is the requirement for a local group separate from the design team, with authority to set point weights and include or exclude certain environmental measures. The tool must be tuned to local conditions before a reasonable assessment can be made.

In addition to the regional flexibility, SBTool is more direct than LEED as it relies less on proxy measures and provides a more transparent framework for discussing environmental options. It has been used in Canada more as a framework for discussing environmental performance and establishing performance targets than as a whole building rating system.

On the disadvantage side, SBTool is still a research product and does not have the benefit of institutional support. Natural Resources Canada no longer directly supports SBTool development. Nor does it offer third-party review (in North America) for assessed projects. If one is looking for public marketing benefits, LEED offers far superior brand recognition.

Q: What were the pros and cons of SBTool?

A: The pros follow closely the arguments above. The cons are too numerous to mention.

- The Excel Spreadsheet format is not well designed or resolved. The worksheets are not easy to debug.
- The environmental measures are very uneven in reporting, with some areas requiring great detail at a fine scale, and others working on gross estimates.

■ The weighting and scoring pages have such a broad range of inputs that they tend to homogenize all scoring. If one decides to prioritize certain performance areas, it is quickly obvious that others with few points can be ignored.

In this case [the Gulf Islands Operations Center] the LEED approach gives a much more equitable position. Similar to the situation where the weighting of the points can homogenize the overall scoring, the energy category of the SBTool also runs into an unintended crossing of supply-and-demand issues. In the LEED assessment, Energy & Atmosphere Credit 1 is used to describe demand management or conservation methods only. Provision of energy through renewable supply is counted in Credit 2. Unfortunately, SBTool lumps all of the energy measures in one category, which then has an aggregated score. The lack of a very large proportion of renewable energy then unduly penalizes the SBTool score on the energy side simply by having a scoring point that is unlikely to be high. A restructuring of the energy section in SBTool would be required to correct the imbalance.

Q: Do you think certain project types are better suited to SBTool or LEED? Do you prefer one over the other?

A: The two systems do very different things. For projects where a strong owner-designer team wants to review performance goals, but then get on with the project, SBTool would provide a good start. For those who want third-party

Figure 12-4 The Gulf Islands Operation Center includes an ocean-based geothermal system and exterior sunshades. *Photo by Derek Lepper. Courtesy of McFarland Marceau Architects Ltd.*

Figure 12-5 The open atrium enhances natural ventilation, and daylight is the primary source of illumination during the day.
Photo by Derek Lepper. Courtesy of McFarland Marceau Architects Ltd.

certification, SBTool is totally inappropriate. Projects looking for marketing muscle should avoid SBTool.

I am getting sick of both tools. My current preference is for post-occupancy evaluations and reconciled energy performance modeling done with current utility bills.

Q: Will your firm recommend SBTool to future clients?

A: For use in discussing performance target only. Not for use as an assessment system on a real project.

RESOURCES

Sustainable Building Information System, www.sbis.info: SBIS is a database launched by the iiSBE to make information on sustainable buildings available to users worldwide. It includes resources on technologies, methods and tools, research and development projects, buildings, and more.

World Business Council for Sustainable Development, www.wbcsd.org: The council is a global consortium of more than 200 companies with the mission "to provide business leadership as a catalyst for change toward sustainable development, and to support the business license to operate, innovate, and grow in a world increasingly shaped by sustainable development issues."[9] Its website offers information related to this mission, including publications and case studies.

World Green Building Council www.worldgbc.org: The World GBC was founded in 2002 by eight national Green Building Councils to "formalize international communications, help industry leaders access emerging markets, and provide an international voice for green building initiatives."[10] The website offers information on establishing a GBC.

NOTES

1. Marie Coleman, Communications Coordinator, USGBC, email to the author, July 17, 2009.

2. Kimberly R. Bunz, Gregor P. Henze, P.E, and Dale K. Tiller, "Survey of Sustainable Building Design Practices in North America, Europe, and Asia," in *Journal of Architectural Engineering*, March 2006, p. 37.

3. Thomas Saunders, "A Discussion Document Comparing International Environmental Assessment Methods for Buildings," BREEAM: 2008, p. 27.

4. HK-Beam Society, "Hong Kong Building Environmental Assessment Method, Version 4/04: New Buildings," HK-Beam Society, 2004, p. 6.

5. www.hk-beam.org.hk/certified/buildings.php; accessed February 23, 2009.

6. www.estidama.org; accessed February 22 and August 1, 2009.

7. Ron Kato, MAICB, LEED AP, Project Architect, McFarland Marceau Architects Ltd., email to the author, July 15, 2009.

8. Ron Kato, email to author, June 25, 2009; and Stephen Pope email to the author, July 15, 2009, reprinted with permission.

9. www.wbcsd.org; accessed February 23, 2009.

10. www.worldgbc.org; accessed February 23, 2009.

INDEX